INSTINCTIVE
SHOOTING
FOR DEFENSE & COMBAT
the Israeli Method

INSTINCTIVE
SHOOTING

FOR
DEFENSE
& COMBAT

the Israeli Method

Fabrizio Comolli
with the SDU Team

4880 Lower Valley Road • Atglen, PA 19310

Other Schiffer Books:
Double Action by Ulrich Schwab (978-0-7643-4630-9)
Modern Knives in Combat by Pöhl & Schultze (978-0-7643-3766-6)
Combat Knives and Knife Combat by Pöhl & Wagner (978-0-7643-4834-1)

Originally published as
Tiro IDC – Tiro Istintivo da Difesa e Combattimento: la Via Israeliana
© 2011 by Libreria Militare Editrice, Milan, Italy.
Translated from the Italian by Ralph Riccio

Library of Congress Control Number: 2017933317

Designed by Justin Watkinson
Type set in Univers LT Std/Minion Pro

ISBN: 978-0-7643-5311-6
Printed in the United States of America

Published by Schiffer Publishing, Ltd.
4880 Lower Valley Road
Atglen, PA 19310
Phone: (610) 593-1777; Fax: (610) 593-2002
E-mail: Info@schifferbooks.com
Web: www.schifferbooks.com

For our complete selection of fine books on this and related subjects,
please visit our website at www.schifferbooks.com.
You may also write for a free catalog.

Schiffer Publishing's titles are available at special discounts for bulk
purchases for sales promotions or premiums. Special editions, including
personalized covers, corporate imprints, and excerpts, can be created
in large quantities for special needs. For more information, contact
the publisher.

We are always looking for people to write books on new and related
subjects. If you have an idea for a book, please contact us at
proposals@schifferbooks.com.

CONTENTS

INTRODUCTION

Before entering into the heart of the technical discussion, following is a brief presentation of the authors and of the structure and the purpose of this book.

Note: Many examples regarding standards, police procedures, etc., refer to the contemporary Italian situation but apply generally to other European countries, and to many other nations in the world, which differ from the USA with respect to the types of firearms, and legitimate defense laws.

The SDU Team

SDU (Security & Defense Unit: לאפר "Raffi G," וזעמש S., וזרחת F.M.) specializes in training in the realm of strategic and tactical security, of defense, and of combat (the Israeli School). The basic mission of the SDU is to prepare with the greatest degree of effectiveness personnel (military, civilian, or various security organizations and services) who might find themselves in critical situations, where the Israeli experience in anti-terrorism scenarios or in unconventional conflicts might prove to be extremely valuable. Unfortunately, this type of scenario tends increasingly to represent the norm rather than the exception. The instruction provided by SDU thus integrates, implements, and perfects a type of traditional training, further developing the potential of each individual operator.

The members of the SDU team have about twenty years of operational activity in security services and specific training in Israel behind them. They also have a specific curriculum as instructors, having completed the rigorous training courses for trainers called for by the Israeli school. They are the only individuals in Italy to have graduated from the company officially recognized by the Israeli Ministry of Defense. This training curriculum offers a wide range of solutions, tailored to different

Figure 1: Members of the SDU team have about twenty years of operational activity in the international arena (security services) and specific training in Israel to their credit.

types of requirements depending on the client: armed forces, police forces, public administrations, security companies, professional operators, companies, commercial enterprises, and private citizens.

In the professional sector, formation consists of training which, without neglecting basic safety rules and procedures for handling weapons, focuses on operational shooting techniques (IDC: Instinctive Defense and Combat) from basic levels to advanced and specialist levels: firing with pistols and rifles, unconventional shooting techniques, individual and tactical techniques working as part of a team, specialization in Tactical/

Figure 2: For more details on SDU activities, see www.sdu-sec.it.

Combat shooting, VIP protection, defense of installations and public places, including tactical and defensive training specifically for aircraft and airport security, and for safety on transportation in general (trains, subways, buses). Course offerings also include special CQB combat, neutralization, and disarmament courses (*krav maga*).

In the civilian/private sector, courses call every level of security situation, from company security to protection of commercial activities at risk, from home defense to personal defense, risk assessment, options for prevention and dissuasion, active defense techniques at all levels including unarmed self-defense (*krav maga*) and armed self-defense (IDC shooting).

SDU has a representational branch office in Milan; courses are given in Italy and (for special full immersion courses) in Israel, but SDU also arranges for ad hoc training throughout Europe and in other countries upon request. The SDU website can be found at www.sdu-sec.it.

For years Fabrizio Comolli has been involved in the development of IDC operational shooting with SDU and collaborates with the team on several projects. He has a background in the humanities (with degrees in philosophy and psychology) and in-depth professional experience in the editorial and communications fields, but also nurtures a strong parallel interest in various aspects of security and personal defense issues.

How to Use This Book

The primary aim of this book is to present the basics of a defensive system, the Israeli system. We wish to present it, illustrating its characteristics and motivations, to offer another tool to whomever has to defend himself with a firearm for private, work, or institutional reasons. We would like it to be clear that when in the book we speak of defense "in the civilian sector" we mean the "civilian scenario" as distinguished from military or high-risk scenarios. The information presented applies to civilians as well as to police or private security forces which operate within national boundaries.

In this book we will illustrate a series of basic techniques that are useful for learning the essential premises of the Israeli method (whose overall technical heritage, obviously, is much more deeply rooted and which would need a number of specialized publications to cover adequately).

Our intent and our hope is that whoever reads this is able to understand this method and, if they wish, to add it to or integrate it with their existing technical expertise. We are not interested in "selling" the method; there is no need for that. Nor is it a sort of "challenge" between different defensive schools of thought; this also is not of interest to us.

We are not here to make comparisons or to say that "This is better than that"; we present the principles and techniques of the Israeli methodology analytically, always explaining the how and why, after which each reader can decide how to assimilate the information in order to improve his own abilities.

It is not our intention to enter into a sterile discussion of the "best," on the position of your feet, the angle of rotation, on being an inch behind or in front of cover, et cetera; those types of discussion are of no interest to us. In this book we wish simply to pass on as clearly as possible the fruits of our experience and of the scientific studies that give life to the Israeli school of defense.

We speak of "defense," but defense against whom? The Israeli method concentrates on defense against terrorists, criminals, thieves, and whomever is bent upon violating the most sacred values, among which is human life. This method was developed in the field, given the critical conditions in which the state of Israel, its citizens, its diplomatic facilities abroad, and the Hebrew communities throughout the world live every day. Everything that you read in this book stems in fact from a very long, intense, and dramatic experience and from careful scientific studies that have been developed and continue to be developed to increase the effectiveness of the techniques and procedures.

The experience to which we refer goes back more than sixty years, in its most obvious and clear version (in 1948 the United Nations officially recognized the State of Israel, and from that day forward there have been almost incessant military and terrorist attacks to which Israel has had to respond), but which is also much more deeply seated; the Israeli DNA is strongly marked by defensive genes developed not only because of current war and terrorism, but also because of persecution of all types and in all places that reached an atrocious high point during the Second World War, and by various types of crimes, theft, and aggression. All of this has always marked the existence of the Israeli people, and has made it necessary, inevitable, and indeed impelling to develop methods of defense. Even before techniques, the Israeli school is based on a common mentality: never again fall victim to violence, never again be the prey. The techniques follow as a consequence. Experience has led to the need for defense, has forced a fighting mentality, has furnished inexhaustible case studies to select and refine the techniques, which are constantly methodically and scientifically updated, tested and improved. In addition, they are intensely tested in the field as part of a tragic daily struggle.

All of this information is gathered together and commented on in order to present both the philosophical and practical principles of the method. That, in short, is the core and sense of the book. We hope that each reader will be open to the information and, if they wish, to accept it.

On the one hand this book is a practical manual that intends to illustrate as clearly as possible a series of techniques for personal defense using a handgun; on the other hand it is a guide on a different and more wide-ranging level that aims at passing on many of the basic principles of the "Israeli way" of defensive shooting.

This two-stage approach stems from an essential rule, which is absolutely the first rule with respect to security, defense, and combat in the Israeli view: the true weapon is the brain; the rest are only tools that are available from time to time. Any weapon is useless if the brain that guides the hand holding the pistol is not prepared and alert. In other words, defense is a question of psychology before it is of technique.

One of the primary features of this book to bear in mind is that here we are not limiting ourselves to a "menu" of different shooting techniques, but instead are devoting ample space to an analysis of the "how" and, most of all, to the "why" of the techniques. There are not that many techniques that are absolutely indispensable to master for personal defensive shooting (but on the other hand they cannot be learned just by reading a manual). The most important objective is to impart the knowledge that is behind all of these techniques and thus the reason why certain techniques have been chosen, refined, and taught. In addition to the operational techniques, an integral part of the learning has to do with handling the weapon safely under all circumstances, and the proper mental approach (managing aggressiveness and stress, etc.). We believe that this book can, in that sense, offer an "added value" that is truly unique.

On the other hand, we are not here to "discover" or invent anything. The Israeli school has used and taught these techniques for decades, with constant refining and updating based on lessons learned in the field and their progressive scientific development.

Thus, this book deals in-depth with the characteristics, the techniques, and the philosophy of the Israeli school, thanks to first-hand and qualified sources. In this book the reader will find not only a series of amply illustrated explanations, but also specific answers to doubts and questions that are frequently heard regarding Israeli operational shooting. The book is thus an attempt to offer a previously unpublished contribution to spreading the word about a particular aspect of defensive shooting.

Along with these factors, the book focuses on a number of technical themes while excluding others. For example, only handguns are addressed, and not long guns such as rifles (which would require a separate treatment in itself). We speak of equipment and techniques that deal only with defensive shooting, but do not address anything that regards other disciplines of competitive shooting, each of which is valid in its own sphere and has its own objectives, but is a completely different matter with respect to an operational approach. The book is structured as follows:

The first part (chapters 1–3) introduces several important baseline ideas: the philosophy and characteristics of the "Israeli way," basic concepts, safety rules;

The second part (chapters 4–9) develops the discussion of operational techniques: shooting techniques, changing magazines, movements, etc.

At the end of the book, chapter 10 addresses the most common questions asked by those who are not familiar with the Israeli method, analyzing in detail and with concrete examples the "why" of several basic procedural choices, techniques, and tactics.

CHAPTER 1

THE PRINCIPLES OF THE ISRAELI METHOD

Before getting to the technical chapters, we believe that it would be very useful to say a few words concerning the philosophy that is behind and at the root of the Israeli method of combat and defense. The techniques and procedures are important, but it is just as important to understand the reasons why; if the techniques and procedures are taught and learned without explaining reasons behind them, they run the risk of being mere gestures, of mechanical movements that have been learned purely in terms of performance. Instead, understanding the reasons upon which the operational choices are based helps us to learn in an intelligent manner and is thus more meaningful and long-lasting.

In addition, as we repeat often in this book, according to the Israeli approach all actions including (and most of all) those associated with combat and defense of human life, are born from and achieve success because of a proper mental attitude, even more than technical and physical ability.

What Is IDC Shooting?

As with any manual that is well-respected, it is useful to agree upon definitions and basic concepts. The shooting method that we will illustrate in this book and that is taught in our courses is called "IDC shooting" or "Instinctive Shooting for Defense and Combat." In the Israeli school these three components are closely connected and integrated: instinct, defense, and combat.

Let's quickly analyze these aspects, to which we will return in a more in-depth treatment later in the book:

Instinct: Instinct, like stress, is an essential "ingredient" of human nature and is an integral component of our psychological structure, especially in situations of sudden danger. It is often an inconvenient component that is sometimes dysfunctional and sometimes invaluable; in general, however, it cannot be ignored or be relegated to the background (to ignore its manifestations or its impulse would be not only tiring and useless, but very risky as well). Let's say that instinct, like stress, is not necessarily our enemy; we have to learn how to recognize it and to use it to our advantage. Instinct represents a very powerful primordial force that must and can be controlled, channeled properly, and managed (but not negated). No one, not even a special forces operator with years of experience, is immune to the pressures of instinct and stress during an encounter; no man is a robot, but rather is a purely rational being. What makes the difference is the ability, honed by training, to face and manage one's instincts, stress, and fear, channeling one's energies into the best organized and effective reaction possible.

Defense: Here we will deal only and exclusively with defensive techniques, never with offensive techniques; armed defense, as we will often repeat, is the last possible and most extreme choice, to employ only when all other alternatives are out of the question.

Combat: To defend oneself does not mean to remain on the defensive, but rather to react and to turn the tables on our aggressor. Defense, according to the Israeli approach, is always active, energetic, and resolute. It is a concept that we will refer to often during the course of this book.

The concepts of defense and combat, in particular, might seem even too obvious; everyone believes (in good faith) to know what it means to defend oneself and what it means to fight. But anyone who has real long-term experience in defense and in combat knows that in fact they are not obvious, and that in that regard many common beliefs should be discredited or corrected. Let us dwell for a moment on that point.

Defense and Combat Shooting

This book is dedicated to defensive shooting which, in our view and in the experience of the Israeli school, is always understood to be combat shooting, or more properly, as combat in the wider sense. Should we then provide a definition of combat shooting? Certainly. Here it is: combat shooting is not definable.

This would seem to be a provocative statement, but it is only minimally so. It is reality. The sporting disciplines are, rightly so, codified, structured, and regulated; sporting achievements have to be measurable and capable of being compared. As a consequence the rules of sporting disciplines are improved by the ability, or better yet by the necessity to clearly define each rule and every technique. Characteristics, caliber, weight, and dimensions of the weapon, types of accessories and clothing, structure of the firing phases, position and type of targets and relative scoring, rules, times, penalty for mistakes, etc.; every aspect of sport shooting is carefully classified and defined.

But defensive shooting (combat) has nothing to do with all of that. Real situations in which a private citizen or a professional operator can find themselves facing when having to defend themselves against a deadly attack are infinitely varied, fleeting, surprising, and chaotic. Is the source of the danger close-by or far away? Visible or not visible? Only one attacker? Two or more attackers? Are we at home? In the office? On the street or in a public place? In a car, train or subway, in an airplane, on a ship? Is the weapon a rod, a knife, a handgun or a rifle, a car, a bulldozer? There are no algorithms, there are no rules or "scientific" formulas that can describe, govern, or help us to automatically resolve this infinite variety of factors and scenarios. This chaotic and unpredictable variety is not the exception, it is the norm in cases of real defense. Thus, even though it might sound paradoxical, the rule is that there are no rules.

But that does not mean, naturally, that one has to surrender to the unforeseen and that one has to adopt an attitude of fatalism. It is obvious that there is a solution (otherwise there would not be thousands and thousands of people in the world who prepare carefully and are able, when called upon, to react effectively against a deadly threat). The essential point, based on our experience, is that to prepare for defense means not to focus purely and simply on techniques, but rather on their "why"; the focus should be on preparing for the psychological aspects before concentrating on procedural and mechanical aspects. Technique is necessary, exercises are useful, the effectiveness of our tools and the speed of our reaction all count, but they are not enough: before all of that, it is indispensable for our mind to be prepared. Our brain, along with our body, is the true weapon and the variable that can decide the outcome of an encounter.

Our mind has to be trained in the proper manner. It has to learn how to recognize situations, potential threats, imminent needs, priorities, and opportunities for reaction. And to prepare itself adequately, our mind has to expand, and not to close itself off.

This is the reason why, in this book, when we present concrete and practical suggestions, we will often add some particular point, some distinction, some cue regarding variations and some critical doubt; we will do it on purpose because each lesson (even partial lessons which a book can teach, and which can never replace hands-on learning under the guidance of expert instructors) must be understood as a stimulus and not as a dogma. Preparing for defense, either armed or unarmed, has to do not so much with learning a sporting discipline as it does with creative problem solving. We need to train ourselves to quickly and intelligently resolve a variety of problematic situations, and to understand how, as we advance in the learning process, this can be extrapolated and extended to any possible

Figure 1.1: Attention to security problems is deeply rooted in the Israeli mentality, given the constant challenge of terrorist threats at various levels.

situation, including and above all those that we do not expect and which violate rules and habits. The aim is to learn and be in control of the unexpected.

The Source: Experience in the Field

The Israeli method of shooting that we define as IDC shooting (Instinctive Defensive and Combat) does not stem from theory but rather from analysis and codification of field experience.

Due to a series of historical reasons, since its beginning Israel has lived in a state of perennial threats against its very security, both at the national and institutional level as well as at the level of individuals and private citizens. Added to this is the constant terrorist threat that hangs over Jewish communities all over the world, regardless of their activities or their nationality. It follows that the resources dedicated and the capabilities developed over the course of time by the Israelis with respect to defense and security are extraordinarily great and probably better than those of any other Western nation, given the exceptional conditions mentioned above (*Figure 1.1*).

In the military field Israel has fought and won numerous wars over the span of a few recent decades. In the law enforcement field the Israeli police forces and intelligence services are faced daily with problems, scenarios, and events of concrete and immediate seriousness, and can boast of a (very dramatic) record in their unceasing series of actions and successes. Numerical data are noteworthy: of a population of some 7–8 million people, there are several hundred thousand armed personnel (including the armed forces, police, various public and private intelligence, and security services). Briefly, the culture of security, of defense, and of combat is profoundly imprinted in the Israeli "DNA" (*Figure 1.2*).

It follows that each methodology and doctrine regarding the subject can point to an immense number of cases and an enormous body of experimental data and extremely detailed critical analysis. Everything that works well is chosen, studied, refined, and passed on to each operator. Vice-versa, anything that does not work, that turns out to be ineffective, or even worse, that causes problems or accidents, is set aside, corrected, or abandoned. This is not an abstract theory, therefore, but an in-depth focus on practical reality, taking into account that any error can have grave consequences.

A first essential point dictated by field experience is safety in handling the weapon, and it should not be surprising: whatever the operator's level of technical expertise might be, use of the weapon cannot and must never ignore a perfect understanding

Figure 1.2: In Israel armed personnel, who protect the country and defend the civilian populace, have a widespread presence and face problems of varying seriousness on a daily basis.

and respect for safety standards and procedures, beginning with basic handling operations to being able to clear a jammed weapon and dealing with unforeseen problems while shooting. A failure to understand or to apply safety rules, dictated by a lack of preparation or by excessive confidence, can set off a chain of errors with very dangerous consequences for the individual, for his companions, and for the whole team. The safety norms of the Israeli school are extremely precise, strict, and complete (the entire protocol includes some fifty rules that are boiled down to "only" about twenty in certain phases of basic training).

Instinct in handling techniques, movement and shooting is, as can be understood by the acronym itself, at the heart of the method. Field experience and studies have enabled techniques to be developed which respect and optimize the spontaneous reaction of body and mind in situations of acute and unexpected stress; holding the weapon, the positions of the body, aiming and transitioning from one target to another, movements in all directions, are all imprinted so as to promote and maximize in the strongest and most effective way possible the psycho-physical reactions of the individual at the moment of danger and time of shooting.

In our training we prefer to leave certain formal aspects in the background and concentrate instead on techniques that are derived from real experience and adapted to real-life operational shooting situations. This is not sport or athletics, but is combat shooting. Real-life situations are diverse, changeable, chaotic, and not programmable like the scenarios of sporting events. In combat the body contracts, the muscles tense, cardiac rhythm accelerates, eyesight and hearing are altered. The target itself, in real combat, is active, reactive, unpredictable in its movements. It is not by chance that in the courses offered by SDU one of the most important and representative components of the training plan is engaging in exercises under stress induced at the psycho-physical level; speed and intensity of reaction, care in assessing the tactical situation and target identification, concentration and judgement ability in the face of uncertain and unforeseen factors, all the while keeping physical fatigue, mental tension, and other unavoidable distracting factors under control.

Combat stress is a key component which cannot be ignored when speaking of defense. It is a subject that is thoroughly covered in several important texts (among which is the classic *On Combat: the Psychology and Physiology of Deadly Combat in War and Peace*, by Grossman and Christensen), so we will not dwell here on theoretical and scientific aspects.

What we do wish to underline, however, is that for operators of the Israeli school, learning is real and concrete, experienced in the field, and is not some fascinating theory learned theoretically or by simulations. A police officer, a soldier, an intelligence operative in Israel is forged in the field, and works as a matter of course and repeatedly in hostile territory, experiences firefights, can find himself under fire from an RPG or a Kalashnikov, learns to fight for his life, for those of his companions, and for the civilians he has to protect, and may have to measure himself with the experience to neutralize an attacker when it is unavoidable. All of this intense and dramatic baggage of experience is constantly analyzed, studied, optimized, and blended into the methodologies and training (*Figure 1.3*).

The Israeli school and the IDC shooting method are based on the fact that this type of training offers the operator (military or civilian, beginner or expert as the case may

Figure 1.3: In Israel coping with deadly security problems in the military and law enforcement spheres is a tragic daily reality.

be) the highest degree of reaction ability, the greatest effectiveness under all circumstances, the highest probability of survival and success for himself and for his team.

The principles of IDC shooting and the Israeli school also represent a model that can be applied in various environments and at various levels; properly speaking, it provides an overall, global approach to defense and combat that addresses unarmed combat, knife fighting, and combat with handguns or long arms. Once the operator has acquired the method, he is able to react and fight at his best under any circumstances and with whatever tool he has available.

Working With an Empty Chamber

One of the peculiar aspects of safety is that operators in the Israeli school work without a round in the chamber (except in special cases). Later in the book we will return often to this topic (both in the technical chapters as well as in the final chapter with essential questions and answers regarding the Israeli method). For now, we will introduce the basic elements, from the philosophical and methodological points of view, of working with an empty chamber (*Figure 1.4*).

This choice affords a very high level of safety, based on our philosophy and our experience, compared to someone who habitually works with a loaded chamber, considering the normal daily activities of the operator (professional or civilian); for example, the risk of dangerous accidents is eliminated, especially at the beginning or end of the day, during pauses, while handling, storing, or drawing the weapon, etc.

Many times during the course of every day the operator picks up his weapon, checks it, loads it, holsters it, unloads it, cleans it, and puts it back in place, and while doing all of this often handles it in the presence of third parties (colleagues, family, bystanders). In all of these circumstances having a round in the chamber poses a great risk; a minor distraction or a trivial error is enough to cause a discharge that is improperly defined as "accidental," and statistics unfortunately demonstrate that this is a risk that is tragically real, and is neither theoretical nor rare.

Based on a large volume of experimental data that has now been abandoned, our own experience has taught us that the speed of drawing the weapon and engagement does not differ in significant measure whether or not there is a round already in the chamber.

Figure 1.4: The Israeli school calls for keeping the weapon with an empty chamber.

Not only that, but the accuracy in identifying and aiming at the target is maximized; the Israeli technique, as we will illustrate in the following pages, calls for drawing the weapon and on racking the slide while focusing eyes and weapon on the target without diverting your gaze for even an instant (as though we were pointing with our finger). Vice-versa, if we were to draw our weapon with a round already in the chamber and with the manual safety on and would have to disengage the safety, you would inevitably lower the focus of your view (no matter how well trained you are, under stress it is almost impossible not to use your eyes to look for the rather small safety catch to disengage it). Briefly, the action of disengaging the safety involves distracting your view of the threat, while the action of racking the slide while drawing the weapon allows the eyes to be kept fixed on the target. There are many private individuals and police officers who carry weapons with a chambered round and the safety on (what is termed "condition one" in the USA). We have made a different choice, that is, no round in the chamber and no safety on, for the reasons we have explained and which we will repeat often in the book. To be sure, there are pistols on the market today that have no manual safety but which are equipped with an automatic safety (firing pin, trigger, etc.), such as the Glock, which in theory can overcome the limitations of the manual safety while still keeping a round in the chamber. From our point of view, however, it is a question of selecting a method, a rule, a behavior to be applied in hundreds or thousands of cases (operators), and when dealing in large numbers the risk factor increases to a level that the Israeli school considers to be unacceptable. The rule has to apply to everyone. Safety is always the first rule, and unfortunately accidents (with a loaded chamber) are always lurking, even for the most expert and best trained shooters. You only have to look at a clip from YouTube searching on "accidental shooting" or similar key words to see some very dramatic examples.

There are of course predictable solutions and specific techniques adaptable to every scenario and eventuality; there are techniques to rack the slide with one hand if the other hand is busy, while carrying objects, while protecting a third person, etc. In addition, remember that we are speaking here of defensive situations in the civilian sector; in other instances, such as during offensive action (checking buildings in a hostile area, searching for dangerous and armed suspects, etc.), one obviously works with a loaded chamber, but these are subjects outside the scope of this book. Certainly in theory there might be situations in which it would be advantageous for someone to have a loaded chamber; the weak hand otherwise in use, an unexpected threat that requires an extraordinarily quick reaction, etc.... But what are the chances that it can happen during our normal life, in the life of a civilian, of an ordinary person? Every day, on the other hand, when a weapon is picked up and stored, a safety check has to be performed, and the need for safe handling thus has a daily and priority value.

Even while keeping strictly to the theme of this book, it is important to understand a basic concept that comes from field experience: a real shooting engagement is very different from whatever might be imagined or from those shown in films. Many myths and distorted ideas have to be debunked.

First: a real firefight is not a duel between gunslingers. This is nothing like the westerns, there are not two opponents who face each other off, look each other in the eye, and who engage in a razor-edge challenge drawing their pistols at the same time in a few fractions of a second. This is movie fantasy. The reality of a modern shooting encounter can be "dirty," confused, and erratic. Perhaps one is in another room and hears a noise, maybe the threat comes from the side, maybe we are getting into or out of a car or the attacker is doing so, maybe we are separated by a staircase, by a wall, by columns, tables, chairs, items in the environment that limit our movement and sight, or the situation is somehow complicated by a host of factors that slow us down or cause doubts. There is nothing at all in common with the perfect and orderly image of a duel.

Let's try to place ourselves in a terribly real situation that has happened repeatedly in Israel in recent times (*Figure 1.5*). We are on the street, in a completely normal civilian setting. Suddenly an attacker shows up driving a bulldozer or bucket loader, hurls himself with the vehicle against innocent passers-by and drivers, intentionally bent on homicide (and in fact, unfortunately, there were many victims). What shooting "techniques" should dictate our armed reaction to save our life and that of other innocent people? What would the importance of being trained to draw, fire, and re-holster a pistol in N seconds be? None at all. What counts here is to be able to quickly assess the situation, to understand how to move, and how to act. The pistol is drawn, the slide is racked to chamber a round, all while thinking quickly, sizing up the threat.

Is the front-end loader stopped or moving? Is the bucket lowered or raised? Is it coming towards us or is it moving away? How can we get close to the driver so that we can act without putting bystanders in danger? And so on. Let's imagine ourselves in a car, bottled up in traffic while the front-end loader is coming towards us. What would be the point of a lightning-fast draw like that of a champion shooter or a gunman from the Old West? The mind should be able to reason quickly, and the right decision might be, if possible, to get out of the car quickly, find some cover, or at least a defilade position with respect to the threat and then, yes, draw and engage to neutralize the danger. The priorities are speed of assessment and tactical evaluation, not the speed of the draw in and of itself. These would be the determining variables for a critical decision in a defensive and combat shooting situation. For this reason we prefer to speak not so much of "combat shooting" but of "combat behavior."

We chose this example on purpose because it is an unusual scenario that is quite surprising but real. And what we want to get across in this book is an awareness that the real circumstances of personal defense are always strange and surprising.

Figure 1.5: In the summer of 2008, a new wave of attacks cast a shadow over the daily life on Jerusalem, using a new method: the weapons used by the assailants were bulldozers or bucket loaders driven at full speed against pedestrians and vehicles. These were surprising and unexpected attacks that appeared suddenly within a completely normal context of road repairs or construction work in the heart of the city. In the space of a month there were three attacks of this type causing a number of dead and wounded. The assailants were stopped, almost always, by armed civilians who were at the scene and who reacted immediately, even before the police could arrive, cutting short the terrorist act and saving other lives that could have been taken.

We initially used the image of a duel because it is emblematic of the ambiguities that are often created in that context, and because it is often implicit (and legitimately so) in some sporting competitions. The disciplines associated with competitive sports shooting are all very nice and inspiring and enable a shooter to refine many important qualities, but we make a distinction between it and the reality of combat which is, unfortunately, a completely different thing, something that is complex, "dirty", and dramatic. For defense and combat shooting our experience has taught us that what counts is to prepare to be reactive and effective under conditions of confusion and surprise. Rather than to put emphasis on concentration and relaxation, in our approach to defensive shooting every exercise has to inject massive doses of surprise and stress. The approaches are different because the objectives are different. The essential element for real-life defense, as we have already stated, is to learn how to deal with the unforeseeable.

In these real circumstances, speed is not a dogma, an axiom, or an absolute and abstract value. In fact, as we have already explained, in some case extreme speed is of no use and can even be harmful inasmuch as it can prevent the proper reading of the situation and identification of the threat. Thus it is useless and mistaken to be fixated on the quickest draw and firing.

Second: a real shooting engagement is not a race against a timer. There is no referee standing next to us ready to time our performance with a chronometer. The considerations in that respect are the same as those we have just set forth regarding the myth of the duel, but we also want to add the concept of timing because, in general, the (obvious) importance of speed is fostered with particular intensity by those who have experience in competitive sports shooting. It is important for us to bear in mind that a real-life shooting encounter is not a shooting competition.

Third: a real-life shooting incident does not have a score. Accuracy is a very important quality when shooting and we always consider it during training. At the same time, we do not concentrate on achieving the "ideal shot pattern" at all costs. Accuracy is just one of the elements of the mix, and we do not consider it in an absolute and abstract way but rather within the overall context. Analyzing the statistics of shooting engagements that have involved security personnel, it has been found that in an actual shooting engagement a tight shot pattern on the target is not a primary factor, nor is it often possible. It is not of primary importance, because in the confusion of combat the most important thing is that the rounds hit the target anywhere. Nor is it possible, most of the time, because, from our point-of-view, during a real-life shooting encounter one cannot concentrate on aiming, the sights cannot be properly aligned to put the rounds on the target with "surgical" precision; that cannot be done because doing so would mean a dangerous delay (we have said that speed should not be worshipped, but is important, and our attacker would hardly stay put and allow us to calmly take aim), and it also cannot be done because our body and our mind prevent it. In fact, combat stress, as amply documented by Grossman in *On Combat*, among various psychological effects, also causes alterations of perceptions such as "tunnel vision" (the gaze fixed irresistibly on the threat) and the loss of depth and three-dimensional perception of the scene. In a real encounter, the only chance and the only real (and realistic) action is to focus clearly on the threat; the wide-open eyes remain focused on the attacker and everything else fades to the point of almost vanishing (always remember that we are speaking about defensive shooting in civilian, everyday scenarios and not of special circumstances such as hostage rescue nor of special forces type personnel). Another reason: the threat, once engaged, is not a static target like a silhouette on a firing range, and so when it is being shot at it moves. In this predicament, clear thinking in evaluating the circumstances and deciding whether or not to assume a new line of fire or to stop shooting counts for even more.

A real shooting engagement is a dramatic and complex event and can have a thousand different facets and unforeseen developments and certainly is never a "clean" and rational event; in order to face it, technical preparation is necessary, but even more so, mental preparation. Reaction speed is certainly important but is not the only variable, nor is it often the main variable. There are many other variables in play, which we will address in this book. In general, we can say that the probability of a firefight is offset by the guarantee of maximum security in daily life; this is the perfect equation.

Attacking the Attacker

An old proverb says: The best defense is an offense. We certainly all know the proverb, but rarely do we stop to think about what it really means (except, perhaps, for an occasional game of football amongst friends). The Israeli school embodies this principle to perfection, has tested it extensively, has witnessed and confirmed its concrete validity, employs it continuously (both in the military as well as in the civilian sector), and pushes it to its extreme limits by virtue of its unequalled field experience.

It is one thing to defend oneself, but it is another thing to be on the defensive. The Israeli method calls for never being on the defensive and never to assume a defensive attitude. Being "defensive" is a passive condition, while "defense" can and should be active. To defend oneself with maximum effectiveness, and thus with the

Figure 1.6: In the Israeli mentality, to defend yourself does not mean to be on the defensive; the only effective defense is one that sees the prey transformed into the predator, the victim attacking the aggressor.

greatest chance of success, the Israeli way calls for reaction with explosive energy, to counterattack the attacker, put him under pressure, to upset the force relation (especially on the psychological level). This principle is applied in all circumstances, both in armed combat as well as unarmed combat (*krav maga*). The implications of this principle affect both the attacked party as well as the attacker.

The attacked party should not feel like a victim and should not accept that role psychologically. An attack, especially in the civilian realm, presupposes an element of surprise. But the person attacked has to instantaneously overcome the surprise and fright, has to overcome his fear, his stress and the adrenaline rush in a charge of energy directed against the attacker. React, fight, counterattack. Transform oneself from the prey to the predator. This, based on our experience, is the key for a winning defense.

The attacker has an initial advantage because he has taken the initiative and has taken the victim by surprise. If the person attacked succumbs to fear and stays on the defensive (paralyzed in place and/or is worried only about finding a way to avoid being hit) the attacker maintains the advantage, and in fact increases it, because as the attack progresses and the attacked party does not react, the mental state of the attacker, his level of violence, his will to overpower, and his predatory instinct becomes more powerful and excited.

On the other hand, if the party that is attacked reacts with the maximum intensity of which he is capable, the attacker is thrown off balance and finds himself facing an unexpected problem. His initiative is broken and, in the most extreme case, the dynamics are reversed because very often an attack is based on the certainty that the victim will be intimidated and terrorized. At times, an attacker puts so much faith in his power to intimidate (whether armed or unarmed) that he does not have a real, deeply rooted mental and technical preparation for combat; in such an instance, the simple fact that the person attacked rebels and reacts with all of his energy and with all that he has learned from serious training can determine the victory of good over evil.

In any event, an attacker who is put under pressure encounters serious difficulties in maintaining his concentration and his psychological (actually, his psychophysical) advantage over the intended victim. The prey which rebels and aggressively counterattacks the predator puts the predator in serious trouble and almost always beats him. It is an infallible rule of nature (think of a small animal that chases off an enormously larger predator by defending its nest, its territory, or its offspring). But it also applies to human beings. There are many examples that can be cited from various situations, ranging from hunting to law enforcement to military operations. For example, let's put ourselves in the shoes of a hunter (the predator): we cautiously approach the prey, we take it in our sights, and we pull the trigger. The prey can be a bird that is in flight or a deer that is grazing and, once alarmed, tries to run away. But if the prey were a large wild boar or an African lion which, put in a corner, suddenly charged us, how would we feel? Would we possibly be shocked by a sudden rush of adrenaline? Wouldn't we for a moment possibly be changed from the role of the predator to that of the prey? Wouldn't we feel pressured, agitated, and in difficulty to be able to aim and shoot, as we would be thrown off balance by the animal's unexpected reaction? The same is true in a military environment; if we are ambushed, the proper reaction is not to go on the defensive, not to run hither and tither to find cover (and thus maximizing our own losses), but to react with a solid wall of fire and by attacking the attackers. Fire and maneuver, fire and maneuver; alternately covering each other, keeping the attackers under pressure and then driving them off.

Later in the book we will return to this important principle. For now we will fix it in our minds as one of the pillars of the Israeli way of defense and combat. Never stay on the defensive. Never remain the prey, always shift from being the prey to being the predator. Never passive, always active and aggressive.

A Context and Style of Life Closely Akin to Those of Europe

Israel is a state that is at the same time ages old and relatively young (from the institutional point of view) but all of its social, political, and legal structures, its lifestyle, its outlook, and its culture are profoundly wedded to Europe. The histories of Europe and Israel are closely intertwined, at many levels.

Without getting into overly deep or complicated analyses, for the purposes of this book we will limit ourselves to considering all that regards the legitimate use of weapons and armed defense in the civilian sector. In this sense the similarities between Israel and countries with restrictive gun laws, as in Europe in general, are notable, while there are notable differences with respect to the situation in the USA (which is often cited as the "standard" reference when it comes to weapons and self-defense). Let's look at a few examples.

From the legal aspect, both Israel and many European and non-European countries are not particularly "liberal" when it comes to the possession and use of weapons by private citizens. There is no norm that can be compared, even vaguely, to the famous Second Amendment to the Constitution of the United States of America (according to which the right to bear arms is a natural and inalienable right of the citizen), which has been upheld by a Supreme Court ruling. As in Europe, and many other countries, both ownership and use of firearms are also strictly regulated in Israel, and it is complicated and difficult to obtain a license to carry a weapon for personal defense; the requirements are very strict and this type of license is granted only very sparingly.

It might seem strange to someone who is not familiar with Israeli reality, but it is so, except for rare exceptions (that have to do with particular circumstances such as some installations and border areas). The reason is that, as we have already said, in Israel security is a vital, primary, and pervasive aspect; there is an extremely high number of armed professional operators (armed forces, police forces, various agencies

Figure 1.7: The laws which regulate the use of firearms are strict, both in Israel as well as in Italy, and a policeman who shoots a criminal is investigated and has to provide proof of his justification. This is an example of a video available on YouTube (www.youtube.com/watch?v=NeFB17CtTww) which shows a police officer who, after having downed an individual who had taken a pistol from a fellow officer and had taken them on as targets, was found innocent thanks only to the footage from street surveillance cameras. This is a good example of both the cultural affinity of Israel and Italy as well as the particular, unique, and tough experience in the field to which Israeli law enforcement officers are constantly exposed.

and services) that watch over the territory in an often discreet but widespread and very effective manner, thus massively reducing the need for an ordinary citizen who is not engaged in a particularly risky activity to go about armed. Very often (and it is always advisable), anyone in Israel who has a license to carry a weapon for self-defense also takes training in proper use of the weapon, which explains why in certain cases (which have been reported in international mass media), among which was the attack using a bucket loader that we have previously described, the intervention by an armed taxi driver, along with the police and special forces, contributed to neutralizing the terrorist act.

Aside from private citizens, in many countries the police forces and many soldiers, in some respects, face situations and limitations much like those of their Israeli colleagues. We have only to cite the famous premise of working with an empty chamber; some European countries have specific directives, regulations, and rules of engagement that mandate that armed government personnel work with an empty chamber, exactly as is the procedure in Israel (which we spoke of at the beginning of this chapter). The "made in USA" approach is quite different, as it calls for the classic loaded chamber and the safety engaged (cocked-and-locked, or condition one).

Still with respect to the law, to fire a weapon even when forced to defend oneself, is not a move to be taken lightly and can have serious legal consequences, in Israel and elsewhere; whether it involves a private citizen or a policeman or even (in some circumstances) a member of the military, whoever fires, even legitimately, is subjected to rigorous investigation and risks heavy consequences unless it can be shown that such an act was fully justified. One has only to look at the Israeli newspapers (www.haaretz.com on the web) or check video clips on Youtube to find numerous examples.

From the social aspect, the lifestyles, the customs, the types of homes all present substantial similarities between Israel and European countries, both in an urban as well as a rural environment. Even construction methods, designs, and materials are generally similar, but different when compared to the United States. In Israel a large part of the population lives in condominiums, small detached houses, or on farms, built in a manner similar to that of corresponding dwellings in Europe; there are no boundless properties such as American or Australian ranches. The walls of Israeli apartments and dwellings are made of solid masonry like European buildings, compared to the prevalent American "light" materials such as wood and sheetrock. Similar considerations apply to doors and windows. These aspects can have a bearing on personal and home defense; let us say that, in general, certain similarities in the social and living aspects can support some similarities between the respective defensive requirements and techniques.

Speaking in general terms, it is well that "important" operational techniques from other countries are carefully evaluated and, as appropriate, modified and adapted, in accordance with the specific characteristics and requirements of our own context.

Two Bulwarks: Security and Human Life

Every decision, every technique, every tactical choice according to the Israeli way must always answer to two basic values, which are linked to each other: security and human life. At times these two values must be balanced between them.

Safety, above all, is the primary concern in all aspects of the use of weapons; as we shall see in a few pages, in a chapter dedicated to it, the safeguard of the safety of an armed operator and of whoever is near him impose a very precise set of rules, procedures, and guidelines. Safety involves the prevention of accidents and involuntary damage (precisely as when we speak of "workplace safety"). We have purposely dedicated an entire chapter to this aspect of security in order to underscore its importance.

Security itself, on the other hand, is defined as "protection" and derives its value from that of human life; every human life is a precious thing to be protected. Every individual has the right to live in safety, and there are those whose job it is institutionally or professionally to guarantee such safety.

In the Judeo–Christian view, as in other cultures and religions, human life is a value that we are obliged to respect, which we cannot dispense with at our pleasure and we must not underestimate whatever threatens it. But if in order to protect a human life, for example, our own or those of our loved ones, we find ourselves having to use a weapon, here is where the value of life runs the risk of running into conflict. The problem has to be thought of beforehand, and not at the crucial moment (hoping obviously that such a moment never happens), because it is a deeply human and ethical decision and not a technical one.

How would we feel if we found ourselves facing an extreme situation? When an innocent party is subjected to a potentially lethal attack, in extreme cases we may find ourselves forced to completely neutralize the threat to save our own lives or that of another person in danger. This eventuality has to be faced up to not only psychologically but also ethically and (for those who are believers) religiously, in addition to legally as well.

Dave Grossman's position in this regard is interesting, in *On Combat* (Chapter 23, "Do Not Kill," or, "Do Not Assassinate"? The Hebrew–Christian view), which we recommend to anyone who wishes to delve further into these feelings.

Looking closely at these two values, security and protection of individual life, they are the basis of Western culture as a whole and of its legal system in whatever form or variation. Let us not forget it and let us not take lightly the implications of armed personal defense.

CHAPTER 2

ABC—SOME BASIC CONCEPTS

Before getting into a detailed explanation of safety norms and shooting techniques, it is worthwhile to define some basic notions which, later in the book, we will take for granted. For the most part these basic notions have to do with our choice of "work tools": the type of weapon, their caliber, their accessories, etc.

For each item, we will provide suggestions that we feel are most appropriate based on experience and (this is very important) which are relevant to the subjects addressed in this book; we do not wish to impart any absolute dogma but rather some principles based on solid grounds. We would remind you that this book deals with defensive shooting with a handgun; in this context we propose solutions which, in a different context, would have to be appropriately modified or adapted.

At the end of this chapter we will add some thoughts on the effects of stress; this is a topic which is potentially vast, although we will refer only to a few aspects.

Criteria for Selection of a Weapon for Defense

In this book we will concentrate on only one type of defensive weapon: the semiautomatic pistol (*Figure 2.1*). That is not to say that other types of weapons, either handguns or long arms, are not suited to defensive shooting in an absolute sense, but here we will concentrate on the choices made by the Israeli school based on field experience gained by operators and by scientific studies to validate, analyze, and further develop those choices.

We thus exclude the revolver from our treatment of the subject. There are those who maintain that the revolver is preferable as a personal or home defense weapon, as it is simpler to use even for people who are not well trained or who are under stress, is able to handle a wide variety of ammunition loads (as its loading cycle does not depend on the power of the cartridge), and is immune to the risk of jamming. It has only a minority of shooters who favor it for defensive shooting, because most experts now agree that the revolver is obsolete or inappropriate for the requirements of real-life operational or defense shooting. We do not wish to take such an extreme position, but do state that our choice falls upon the semiautomatic pistol for a number of practical reasons. Their simplicity, immediacy of use, and handling argue in favor of the more modern semi-auto pistols (considering for example several objective disadvantages of the revolver: significant weight and size of models with long barrels, recoil forces of snub nose models, excessive stiffness of double-action trigger pull, and excessive lightness of single-action trigger pull, etc.). Also arguing in favor of the semi-auto are cartridge capacity (the number of rounds in a staggered row magazine is double or triple that of a revolver's cylinder) and ease of reloading (there is no comparison between changing magazines and emptying and reloading a cylinder).

We also exclude long arms (rifles, carbines, and shotguns) from our treatment of defense shooting, even for home defense. From a practical standpoint, using a carbine or rifle inside a house or apartment has its own set of problems such as handling the weapon in a somewhat confined space, overly powerful ammunition, recoil, noise, and muzzle blast that can disturb the shooter, especially at night in the dark, etc. For these reasons, generally speaking we do not advise the use of a long gun for personal defense. By the same token, it is obvious that such a choice could be justified under certain circumstances. If you only own a rifle, by necessity, you would have to learn how to use that weapon for defensive purposes; if you live on a farm that is isolated and has a large amount of empty land around it a long gun can offer a tactical advantage, etc. Let's just say that, under normal urban and civilian scenarios that we deal with in this book, the preference is for handguns rather than long guns, without interpreting the use of a long gun as a taboo. We leave a discussion of the use of a long gun to another venue, which would require ample time and space as a separate subject.

Among semiautomatic pistols, we prefer models without a manual safety (such as the Glocks) or those that are fitted with a simple hammer safety (as on many SiG Sauer models). As always, we do not want to endorse a specific make or model of weapon, but wish to underscore a principle. Principles are always valid, while their application and specific cases (the models of weapons) can change over time. The principle in this case is simplicity.

Figure 2.1: Among the unending variety of long arms and handguns, our choice for defense shooting is the semiautomatic pistol.

A manual safety can be the cause of a thousand problems in real-life defense shooting. It forces us to take an added step before opening fire, a step which, even though unwillingly, leads inevitably to lowering our gaze (an instinctive move, especially when under stress) and thus losing sight of the threat itself. It can also be engaged involuntarily and inadvertently while racking the slide (to chamber a round or to clear a jam). There are documented cases, which are cited in Grossman's *On Combat* of agents who fell in action, and were found scattered on the ground all of the rounds from the magazine, unfired. The weapon had jammed and the agent, under the extreme stress of a live-fire engagement, had racked the slide to eliminate the problem. While racking the slide the safety had been engaged and when the trigger was pulled the weapon only went "click." The agent, thinking that the weapon was still jammed, had mechanically repeated the action, continuing to rack the slide and thus ejecting all of the perfectly good rounds one after another until he was left with a completely empty weapon and meeting a fatal end.

To work a manual safety (*Figure 2.2*) requires awareness and precise control of one's movements, the so-called fine motor skills; these are requisites that do not mesh well with psychophysical stress conditions that mark a real-life encounter. Modern weapons are designed and manufactured with materials, technologies, and mechanical solutions that are able to guarantee total reliability. There is no longer any theoretical justification for a manual safety (whose continued existence often depends on a design philosophy and, we might say, a stylistic philosophy as well).

Figure 2.2: The manual safety is very difficult to use under stress and can be the source of serious problems in a combat setting. *Note*: The choice of the two weapons illustrated is merely an example and implies no judgement as to merit (as we specify from the outset in the book).

A de-cocking lever has a different function than that of a manual safety: it lowers the hammer to the rest position after a round has been chambered. This allows the weapon to be handled with complete safety (the lowered hammer is not in direct contact with the firing pin; it is usually kept at a distance by a mechanism that is actuated only by trigger pressure) but, at the same time, is available for immediate use. When the hammer is lowered, the pistol can fire in the double-action mode; that is, by simply pulling the trigger the hammer is armed and then hits the firing pin. This means that, while rapidly racking the slide, even if the de-cocking lever were to be involuntarily engaged it would not compromise firing the weapon.

The Best Caliber for Defense Shooting

Each pistol caliber has its own reason for being, as does, in general, every handgun or long gun caliber, depending on the purpose and context of their use (*Figure 2.3*). For shooting with a handgun the smaller calibers allow very accurate firing and thus are ideal for competitive target shooting (think for example of Olympic shooting based on .22 and .32 calibers). The very large pistol calibers, on the other hand, offer too much power and are used, where allowed, as in the USA, for hunting or for shooting metal targets, etc.

In this book we deal exclusively with operational defense firing, and thus concentrate on selection of the most suitable caliber, according to our assessment and our experience. Having thus already discussed selection of the semiautomatic pistol, we will turn our analysis to the relative calibers, excluding revolver calibers.

Based on our experience, 9 mm—that is 9x19 mm or "9 Luger" (which is widespread throughout the world)—is the caliber that at this time offers the following characteristics in a well-balanced manner:

    Power/effectiveness
    Handling
    Ammunition capacity
    Cost considerations

Figure 2.3: Various common calibers for handguns and long arms.

Let us examine these subjects one by one.

Power/effectiveness: The power and effectiveness of 9 mm ammunition is more than adequate compared to both smaller and larger calibers. Calibers smaller than 9 mm, for example 7.65 mm (.32 caliber), are now considered obsolete and/or ineffective for defensive and operational shooting (except for rare occasions in particular circumstances). The discussion is different when it comes to calibers larger than 9 mm, such as .40 caliber or (even better) .45 caliber. In truth, .40 caliber was developed mainly for sporting use, in the framework of Dynamic Shooting, in order to achieve a mix of power and rate of fire that could offer a competitive advantage, based on that sport's discipline; for that reason we do not consider it when discussing "operational" calibers in the strict sense. The real, great, arguable comparison is always between 9 mm and .45 caliber; which of the two is more effective? For effectiveness we mean, briefly, the so-called "terminal ballistics," or the effect produced by the impact on the target; in terms of defense shooting we are talking about stopping power, which is the ability to more or less immediately stop an attacker. To stop an attacker in his tracks (who may be having an adrenaline rush or may be under the influence of drugs), what would be better, a "fast and light" (9mm) bullet or a "slow and heavy" (.45 caliber) bullet? The argument over the "best caliber" is virtually endless, as is a discussion between fans of any particular sport, and fills pages and pages of magazines and books. Fans of the 9 mm and fans of the .45 caliber set forth examples, real cases, and test demonstrations. Some cite cases of shootouts in which 9 mm performance was inadequate, while others object and cite cases to the opposite and the choice of that caliber by operational units and special forces of various countries. Many experts have studied the effects on a target using ballistic gelatin (an artificial gel with characteristics very similar to those of the human muscle mass); others respond that a human body consists not only of muscle mass and that therefore such tests have only a limited value, and so forth.

We do not wish to enter into the merits of these arguments because we feel that the subject should be viewed in a broader perspective. On the one hand, we will limit ourselves to provide advice based on our experience and operational experience of the Israeli school, which makes its choices based on responses from the field and not on mathematical theories, personal preferences, or on the latest fad.

The 9 mm has been adopted for years by Israeli professionals in all walks (military, law enforcement, and private citizens). Among other considerations, two of the episodes that supported the adoption of the 9 mm were the incidents at Fiumicino and Vienna, where several terrorists were hit repeatedly in various parts of their bodies, but not in vital areas by Israeli agents who were using 7.65 mm weapons; following those dramatic events, based on specific studies, it was found that the probability of stopping an attacker by hitting him in non-vital areas with the 7.65 mm round was less than half when compared to the 9 mm round. On the other hand, the reasons for this choice, when keeping in mind the real use of the weapon, cannot be limited to the question of "power" in the abstract; the power of the caliber is only one of its characteristics. There are others that weigh heavily in overall performance, such as those that we will now look at.

Handling: Pistols chambered for 9 mm are more compact, lighter, and easier to handle than the .45 caliber, and thus are easier to carry and handle by anyone, male or female, despite differences of overall body size, hand size, physical strength, etc. Recoil is slightly less and thus easier to control. Even the return springs, which offset the movement of the slide, are generally weaker and thus it is easier to rack the slide to chamber a round or to clear a jam.

Ammunition capacity: Pistols chambered for 9 mm generally offer, for reasonably compact dimensions (see above), a significant ammunition capacity thanks to staggered-row magazines that hold fifteen or more rounds. The legends and "statistics" should be debunked according to which (as is often heard) an average of less than five rounds are fired in a shootout; the reality is that in the unfortunate event that a weapon has to be used, a good supply of ammunition can be far from superfluous. As we have already mentioned, there are .45 caliber pistols available with staggered row magazines but that are not suitable for everyone; only a person with a large body and with adequate training can comfortably carry and be able to handle such a weapon, but it cannot be considered an appropriate choice for most individuals. On the other hand, even a person with those kinds of characteristics can use a 9 mm pistol just as easily as anyone else.

Cost considerations: The 9 mm is considerably less expensive (both to buy as well as with respect to ammunition) compared to .40 or .45 caliber, which is somewhat important. In fact, we would like to stress that the economic aspect should not be underrated, as it is closely connected to the intensity and frequency of training. Not everyone has ample financial resources and shooting is a costly activity; weapons are costly, range time is costly, and ammunition, is also costly. It is useless to choose a large-caliber weapon, which in itself may be quite expensive, and then use it rarely because its ammunition costs too much. This would lead to a situation in which a person would not be able to use it effectively in a moment of need. Serious and ongoing training is indispensable and required for anyone who owns a weapon; consequently, even the costs of maintaining it, and in particular the cost of ammunition, although not a determining factor, should be taken into consideration.

Summary: The choice of caliber cannot and should not be based on an abstract presumption of power as an end in itself; what counts is overall performance which includes, in addition to power, other characteristics such as overall ease of handling, magazine capacity, and low cost (which allows regular training to be conducted). Even admitting that a large-caliber bullet that is slow and heavy might be slightly more effective than a lighter bullet, its real effectiveness will be zero if it misses the target (because the shooter is not able to deal with the recoil and put more than one shot on target) or if the magazine is empty because of the limited number of rounds it can hold, and so on. Considering all of these aspects, we advise adoption of the 9 mm caliber.

There is a famous proverb that makes the rounds of shooters throughout the world, but most of all in the USA where there is a lively "rivalry" over calibers and type of weapon. The proverb states that the ideal is to own two pistols: "A .45 caliber Colt 1911 to show your friends and a 9 mm Glock to show your enemies." It is a cute saying which, in our opinion, makes an important point: in our choice of weapon and caliber, we should not give in to purely aesthetic or emotional criteria but must instead bear in mind more rational factors. If a particular weapon strikes our desire as a collector or for sporting reasons, and if we can afford it, that's fine, but when we have to choose the weapon that we will use in service, for work, or to defend ourselves or our loved ones, we should think carefully about what we have discussed in these pages.

Accessories, Gear, and Clothing

With respect to the choice of holsters, magazine pouches, and other accessories, there is not much to say; it is a good idea to consider types that are essential, functional, or "operational" and forget about everything that is too sophisticated, too complicated, and which is dedicated to competition shooting. The holster has to be compact, comfortable, and easy to use. For the needs of defense shooting either an internal or external belt holster is advisable, that is, a holster worn either inside or outside the trousers, but in either case thin and sticking close to the body (*Figure 2.4*). Whoever, for service reasons, has to use issue equipment should bear in mind that the principles and technical rules that we will now present are still useful, but naturally will require an intelligent adaptation to the situation and use of the items available.

The holster should hold the weapon so that the trigger guard is covered (so that the trigger finger cannot accidentally make contact with the trigger), has to hold the weapon with enough pressure so as to not allow it to shift while running, jumping, rolling, or making other abrupt movements, and is worn on the strong side, that is, on the side of the hand that will hold the weapon. It is useless for us to suggest specific models, as long as these basic principles are kept in mind.

Figure 2.4: The ideal holster is strong but simple.

Based on our experience and the requirements for operational defense shooting (think of a civilian or a plain-clothes officer) we feel that we should discourage the use of the following types of holster:

High-technology holsters that are complicated and which protrude; the ideal holster should ensure that the weapon is properly held but it should be very simple and, we might say, almost rudimentary. Anything that is complicated and/or increases the size of the holster is not good because it creates a useless encumbrance, increases the visible profile of the weapon and, potentially, hinders extraction under emergency conditions.

In particular, holsters fitted with special systems that enclose or hold the weapon: there are holsters which, to maximize the ability to firmly hold the weapon (against the risk of loss or having it removed by someone else) use laces or flaps that have to be unbuttoned, or mechanical systems which, during the

 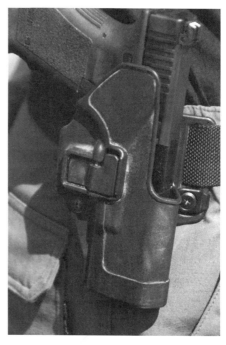

Figure 2.5: Holsters with restraining systems to lock the weapon in place are not used by the Israeli school because under stress and in actual operational scenarios they can cause serious problems while drawing the weapon.

draw, have to be deactivated by finger pressure or by a distinct voluntary movement (*Figure 2.5*).

Such holsters can be adapted to carry the weapon while wearing a uniform, but not for concealed defense purposes, inasmuch as the action of unlocking can cause the draw to be slowed down in an emergency situation and, most of all, runs the risk of making it very difficult under the effects of acute stress, typical for a defensive reaction, and inhibiting the fine motor movements of the hands and fingers (see *On Combat*).

Shoulder holsters and in general, cross-draw holsters; cross-drawing slows down reaction time, requires movements that are superfluous and disadvantageous to aiming and firing (the arm goes in one direction, and then when the weapon is in the hand, goes in the opposite direction, causing significant oscillation and shaking) and exposes the shooter to serious risk in close combat. In fact, we stress that when we speak of defense shooting we are referring to a combat situation in the widest sense of the word; in a true combat situation there is no clear distinction between armed and unarmed combat, there is no neat simulation and so on, the attacker can be in very close proximity to us to the point that he is in physical contact, there can be other persons who get between us, bump into us, grab hold of us due to panic, etc. When our arm crosses our chest in order to draw the pistol from the opposite side, if someone puts any pressure (even relatively slight) on our arm it could immobilize it completely against our abdomen, preventing us from drawing the weapon, and putting us in a position that is dangerously exposed to various types of attack (*Figure 2.6*). Those who defend the cross-draw method maintain that it allows the weapon also to be drawn with the non-dominant hand which (even though not very easy to manage) offers a backup solution in case the strong hand cannot be used; if, however, we consider a real-life situation, the only reason why we cannot use our strong hand is that it was wounded or rendered unusable (any other impediment could be removed if the weapon had to be drawn; the grasp on a surface providing support would be released, an item being carried would be dropped, a person would be pushed out of the way, etc.) which means that the fight is already in progress and that the attacker would hardly allow us to draw our weapon, relatively more slowly and laboriously, with our weak hand while he remained passive and waited. In any event, it is quite improbable that a situation would arise that meets all of these conditions (strong arm unusable and the ability to draw with the weak

Figure 2.6: To carry the weapon in a cross-draw position, that is, on the weak side, could expose us to various risks, especially in the case of a scuffle; the aggressor finds himself in a particularly favorable position to grab our weapon or to hinder our draw.

hand with no impediments), and our experience teaches us that it is advisable to be prepared as best we can for the most usual and statistically probable situations, in the unfortunate case of need, and be able to react accordingly.

For a professional operator, we believe it is advisable to have two spare magazines in a double magazine pouch. For a civilian, in a normal daily context, one spare magazine should be more than sufficient. Remember that the Israeli school is rooted in an operational context in which multiple terrorist threats with a high degree of firepower make it necessary not to be stingy with ammunition.

The ideal magazine pouch, based on the same principles that we set forth for the holster, is extremely simple; it should be comfortable, light, and able to be attached to the belt firmly and securely. Like the holster, the simpler and smoother it is the better it will serve its purpose, among other things, minimizing the risk of snagging on clothing.

It should hold the magazines simply by friction and should not have any strange or complicated mechanisms (for example, for our type of use, pseudo-scientific magazine pouches with joints, springs, and various gears should be completely avoided), nor should they have any flaps, covering, or closure of any type, and it is essential that the pouch is secured to the belt by solid fixed loops rather than by spring clips that run the risk of slipping in case of intense, sudden real-life use (*Figure 2.7*).

The pouch is worn on the side opposite the holster, in a position that can be easily reached by the weak hand.

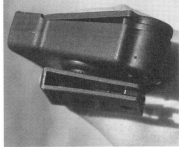

Figure 2.7: The twin magazine pouch, like the holster, has to be simple. Certain types of overly sophisticated magazine pouches are no good because they are too complicated and delicate and because their method of securing to the belt does not stand up well in real use. In use under stress it often happens that these types of magazine pouches end up in the hand of the shooter or fall to the ground during a quick magazine change. It should be noted that the leather magazine pouch (on the left) was originally fitted with a retaining flap with snap closures that was removed completely (cut off) to make it usable effectively and safely.

Other than the holster and the magazine pouch, no other particular accessories are needed. Gun-mounted lights or lasers are very nice accessories that are technologically advanced and which are useful in certain professional situations, but in our opinion are not an indispensable item (and in fact can have some negative aspects) for civilian and home defense use.

The clothing we wear should be comfortable and allow sufficient ease of movement, should not disclose the fact that we are armed, and must allow a rapid draw in case of need.

In the fall and winter long jackets that reach down to the buttocks (three-quarter length coats) are preferable to short jackets (which, when the arms are raised, would expose the belt line and show the holster and magazine pouch) or to overcoats (which, if buttoned, would make drawing the weapon very difficult). The ideal is to leave the front of the jacket open or to choose a type that can be left partly unbuttoned in the front; the closure could be buttons, automatic, or even a zipper, as long as the zipper has a double slider (that allows the top part of the jacket to be closed while the bottom part of the zipper can be opened). This allows a fold of the jacket to be lifted to grasp the weapon. The same principles apply to spring and winter clothing, consisting of light jackets or coats (*Figure 2.8*).

When we are not wearing a jacket or coat, the weapon can be concealed under a sweater, a sweatshirt, a shirt, or even a T-shirt worn outside the trousers; if required, the weak hand can raise the edge of the sweater while the strong hand draws the weapon (*Figure 2.9*).

Acting (and Reacting) Under Stress

Now that we have discussed some basic aspects concerning tools and materials, we will close this chapter by recalling several equally essential (in fact, even more important) notions that regard software rather than hardware; that is, the psychological and psychophysiological aspects. Our body and our minds are our true tools, they are the heart and the pivot point of our every action (or reaction) and our survival depends on them. All the rest, including weapons and accessories, are only the means to be used according to the circumstances.

Defense against an attack hardly ever occurs in the linear, clear, precise conditions described in courses and manuals; neatness and abstract techniques are the result of simplifications and teaching requirements, but reality is quite another thing. It is

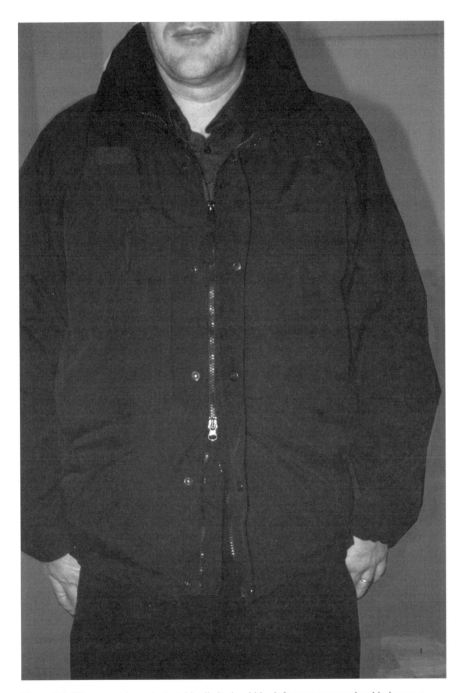

Figure 2.8: When wearing a jacket, ideally it should be left open or you should choose a type that can be left partly unbuttoned in front; the fastener can be buttons, snap closures or even a zipper, as long as the zipper has double sliders (that allow the jacket to be closed on top but that can open the bottom portion of the zipper itself).

Figure 2.9: To draw the weapon while wearing a shirt or a sweater outside the trousers, lift the garment with the weak hand while the strong hand grasps the weapon.

of little use to learn dozens of techniques if they cannot then be applied. Techniques are useful, certainly, but at the crucial moment there are other factors that determine victory or defeat. These factors are not of a technical, but rather of a psychological (and psychophysical) nature and are closely related to stress. The first deadly enemy in combat is stress, which can disorient and paralyze. But stress can also be a powerful ally. In any event it would be very dangerous to ignore it, and in fact we need to learn to understand it well.

Let's imagine ourselves in a state of rest and relaxation, to the point of being distracted; we are taking a walk, watching TV, chatting with someone, or thinking of our own business. Suddenly someone attacks us. It is an armed attacker, clearly bent on doing us harm.

In a few fractions of a second our body organisms are subjected to a sort of chemical and nervous explosion; we experience an adrenaline and testosterone rush, our heartbeat rises precipitously and our breathing becomes rapid. Specific functions of the nervous system become activated (in particular, the sympathetic nervous system), our behavior tends to escape rational and conscious control, and a number of bizarre psycho-perceptive phenomena manifest themselves (changes in vision, hearing, and other bodily functions). In brief, we find ourselves subject to an attack of acute stress, the stress of combat or, as defined more generally, the stress of a critical event.

The intensity of stress and the corresponding activation or excitement of our organisms (heartbeat rate and related psychological phenomena) can be divided into various levels or phases. Each level corresponds to a certain grade of effectiveness of our mind-body system: up to a level of medium or medium-high stress this effectiveness tends to increase. Even though we lose control of some "precision" functions, in compensation we gain increased efficiency in "emergency" functions. Then, as the stress continues to increase, we reach a level where our capacity to react decreases drastically, to the point of complete defenselessness.

These phenomena are well known to anyone who is professionally engaged in defense and combat, but have been developed in outline form and been popularized with particular success by several experts; famous in this respect, among others, are two personalities of note in the US military and law enforcement sector, Jeff Cooper and Dave Grossman (who in turn have borrowed from or collaborated with other well-known specialists, but who themselves are credited with having refined and publicized these concepts to a large audience with great effectiveness). Jeff Cooper, who is also known as the father of practical handgun shooting or dynamic shooting, introduced a color code to identify the various levels of psychological activation: from Condition White (total unawareness) to Condition Yellow, Red, etc. Cooper referred exclusively to the state of mind. Dave Grossman, on the other hand, in the celebrated book *On Combat* to which we have previously referred several times, developed and extended that model, drawing on the studies of other authors, and proposes an outline that also includes physiological aspects (heart rate and sensory and perceptive effects). We have reproduced this outline developed by Grossman because it is a very useful practical reference (*Figure 2.10*).

Condition White corresponds to a state of total relaxation and lack of attention or awareness; in this condition we are not aware of what is happening around us and are not capable of reacting quickly to an attack. Condition Yellow is relaxed alertness; we are busy with something else but are able to perceive what is happening around us and are thus able to react to an unexpected threat. Animals, for example dogs, live constantly in Condition Yellow; always moving and alert, ready to shift in an instant from play to fighting, from happiness to aggressiveness, quick to flee or to attack. In Conditions White and Yellow the heart rate remains at normal levels and there are no changes in perception or motor skills.

Notes:
- The effects described here refer to the increase in heart rate determined by hormonal causes or by fear, by activation of the sympathetic nervous system. Similar increases in heart rate induced by physical exercise do not have the same effect.

- The performance and strength levels induced hormonally can reach their maximum level within a span of ten seconds, then drop fifty-five percent after thirty seconds, thirty-five percent after sixty seconds and thirty-one percent after ninety seconds. Three minutes of rest are needed to "recharge" the system.

- An extended period of relaxation following an intense activation of the sympathetic nervous system can give rise to a parasympathetic collapse, with a sharp decline of energy level, heart rate, and blood pressure. This collapse can manifest itself as normal shock symptoms (dizziness, vertigo, nausea, vomiting, clammy skin) and with a profound state of exhaustion.

(Chart and captions taken from *On Combat*).

Heart Rate
Beats Per Minute

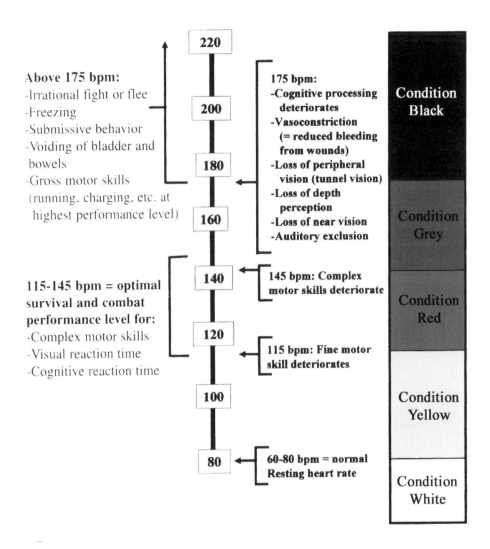

Above 175 bpm:
-Irrational fight or flee
-Freezing
-Submissive behavior
-Voiding of bladder and
 bowels
-Gross motor skills
 (running, charging, etc. at
 highest performance level)

175 bpm:
-Cognitive processing
 deteriorates
-Vasoconstriction
 (= reduced bleeding
 from wounds)
-Loss of peripheral
 vision (tunnel vision)
-Loss of depth
 perception
-Loss of near vision
-Auditory exclusion

115-145 bpm = optimal
survival and combat
performance level for:
-Complex motor skills
-Visual reaction time
-Cognitive reaction time

145 bpm: Complex
motor skills deteriorate

115 bpm: Fine motor
skill deteriorates

60-80 bpm = normal
Resting heart rate

220
200
180
160
140
120
100
80

Condition
Black

Condition
Grey

Condition
Red

Condition
Yellow

Condition
White

Figure 2.10: Effects of hormonal or fear induced heart rate increase.

When we find ourselves unexpectedly in danger, we enter into Condition Red. Condition Red is that of extreme stress, in the midst of an attack. The heart rate increases to between one hundred beats per minute to more than 150. There is a loss of control of precision motor movements, the so-called fine motor skills (such as movement of the fingers to manipulate small objects), which can manifest itself by a certain tremor, but the performance abilities of complex motor skills (coordination between various parts of the body, for example the arms and legs) are maintained or in fact are enhanced, as well as the speed in executing movements and speed of perception and of thought; in brief, at this level the mental and physical abilities that can influence flight or fight reactions are maximized. As stress continues to increase, Conditions Grey and Black are reached, systems reactions become more intense and progressively uncontrollable. When heart rate surpasses the 150 beats per minute threshold, complex motor abilities are lost and only the capability for vigorous but clumsy movement, mostly symmetrical in nature, is retained; raising or lowering both arms, running, etc. Perceptions are noticeably altered. Vision is restricted or hindered; tunnel vision manifests itself (focused on the threat, on the attacker's weapon, and on the hand holding the weapon), near sight decreases or disappears, and depth perception is lost. Hearing can be inhibited (all noises may be attenuated or may not even be heard) or, to the contrary, exaggerated (all noises seem to be greatly magnified). The sense of time is distorted; everything seems to happen in slow motion. And the list goes on. There are also changes of some basic physiological functions, such as pain perception (which is often minimized or even absent during a fight) and even bleeding (in some cases blood does not begin to flow from the wounds until after the action is over and the subject has relaxed).

We refer the reader to *On Combat* for a more in-depth discussion on critical event stress and its very important implications, but here we would like to extrapolate and summarize those aspects, that is those typical perceptual and motor changes, which have a direct relevance for us regarding the subject of armed defense and the techniques of the Israeli school (although some basic principles are shared by many other combat schools).

Symmetrical position, contraction of legs and shoulders: in response to a sudden fright, in an instinctive alarm reaction, the body tends to assume a symmetrical position and to close in on itself to some degree; the muscles contract, the legs bend (ready to jump), the head lowers into the shoulders, and the arms stiffen. The Israeli school does not attempt to fight these instinctive reactions, but instead teaches how to take advantage of them. The position that is assumed to draw the weapon and open fire in fact corresponds with these characteristics; a stable position, normally frontal, full of energy, with the legs bent and the arms pointed straight towards the threat, as if to point to it or to strike it physically.

Eyes wide open: due to the emergency stress, both eyes tend to remain open and fixed on the threat. The Israeli school teaches to shoot with both eyes open instead of closing one to take aim (except for particular cases). Defense shooting is essentially instinctive shooting, pointed rather than aimed.

Tunnel vision: stress leads to restricting vision, focusing only on the threat, in particular on the attacker's weapon. The gaze is usually fixated on the pistol or knife of our attacker and loses sight of a large part of the surroundings. This is an instinctive but damaging reaction; it is difficult to resist, but we nevertheless have to try to overcome it or at least to limit its effect. For this reason it is advisable not to aim by closing one eye, which would halve a field of vision that is already restricted and compromised but (as we have just said) rather to keep both eyes wide open in order to gather in as much as possible within your field of vision.

Loss of fine motor skills: stress reduces or removes the ability to make precision movements with your fingers. For this reason, the Israeli school discourages the use of holsters with complicated mechanical retaining devices, as it also advises against using pistols with manual safeties. Under stress it becomes very difficult to unfasten the holster lock or to disengage the safety, all motions that slow us down, oblige us to lower our gaze, or which actually fatally compromise our defensive reaction.

In general, many techniques and procedures taught by the Israeli school are based on the fact that under stress, perceptions and movements are altered; the manner of holding and using the weapon, the double-check (visual and by touch) during a safety check, and many other rules stem from practical experience garnered from those who, by profession and/or their entire lives, face and understand the stress of combat.

In addition to these considerations we would add that stress can be:

Prevented, thanks to appropriate training. Training in defense techniques with realistic methodologies and exercises that call for induced stress help to prepare us not only technically but mentally and emotionally as well. We can "vaccinate" ourselves against stress to some extent by being subjected to stress under controlled conditions under the guidance of expert instructors.

Managed, thanks to self-control. In the heat of action, in order to offset the harmful effects of stress, we can try, when we have an opportunity, as for example when we find ourselves behind helter for a moment, to calm down and regain our normal breathing (in *On Combat*, for example, the so-called Tactical Breathing is described).

Studied, thanks to debriefing. In the phases immediately following a critical event (such as a shootout that had just ended) and even after a few days or a few weeks have passed, it is very important to remember and to analyze everything that happened, along with any other people who were involved and with the support and guidance of qualified persons (doctors, psychologists, etc.).

The Three Circles of Security

To speak of defense shooting means to speak of security, and the Israeli vision of security is broad and well-articulated. When thinking of how to provide security (public, personal, of loved ones and of one's property), it would be very limiting and mistaken to focus only on an armed reaction, which is really the extreme case, the last step (which we should avoid at all costs); before reaching that point, there are preliminary security levels to put in place and guarantee. In general, we consider security to be a system consisting of three levels or three phases (*Figure 2.11*):

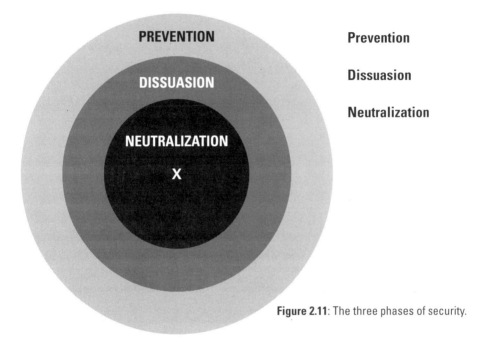

Prevention

Dissuasion

Neutralization

Figure 2.11: The three phases of security.

Why are three phases represented by three circles? Let's keep in mind the image of three concentric defense perimeters, as for example three circles of walls surrounding a city; the first circle is the largest outer circle, and the other two are further inside and are smaller. The further in the circle, the closer the enemy has come to the heart of our city; to the contrary, the farther out the circle is, the further the enemy is being kept at bay.

Prevention is the first level of security. To prevent means to foresee the danger and avoid any contact with the threat, in fact, to even allow the threat to present itself. Prevention is based on intelligence, on the gathering of information, on knowledge of the territory and of the environment in which we move, on the identification and elimination (or limiting as much as possible) of the risk factors.

Prevention means, for example, not to park in dark and isolated places, to set up effective passive defenses of our home and surrounding grounds (gates, strong doors, perimeter alarms, etc,), but not only that. In a more general sense there exists what is termed as behavioral prevention, a very broad subject which departs from the specific discussion of defense shooting but which is nevertheless important; it is a question of developing a mentality oriented towards security: avoiding an excessive show of wealth (jewelry, watches, money), to be aware of people and of your surroundings so as to notice suspicious activity or various indicators of danger, and so on. This is not the place to get into a deep and detailed discussion of this subject, but it is advisable to bear in mind that this is the first, broad circle of security that we should set up around ourselves and that which we wish to defend. As the proverb says, an ounce of prevention is worth a pound of cure, especially when we speak of risks of harm and human life.

A second level, the next circle, is **dissuasion**. In simple terms, dissuasion consists of raising the cost of a potential attack to the point that is not worth the price, and that it may even be disadvantageous or even harmful to the attacker. When the risk or cost of a criminal action is perceived as greater than the possible gain, the attacker gives up the idea (unless he is in an altered mental state due to psychological problems or because of alcohol or drugs). Dissuasion is not only a passive defense (as is prevention); it is the prospect, the anticipation, or the potential for an active reaction ("every action has an equal and opposite reaction…," a bit like the laws of physics). Dissuasion is an intermediate step which, in a passive mode (environmental objects and factors) or active mode (behavior and communication) keeps the threat at arm's length and prevents it from being put in motion. Let's keep this principle in mind: never be the prey.

When dissuasion fails to work, the threat reaches into the heart of our defenses, and has to be confronted at the third and innermost level; the level of **neutralization**. If it has not been possible to prevent the attack, if we have not been able to dissuade the attacker before he acted, we will find ourselves forced to actively neutralize him. Neutralizing an attacker is the objective of the defense techniques (armed or disarmed, depending on the circumstances). It is at this level that the IDC shooting method described in this book fits in. When it is necessary to neutralize an attacker we have to do it in the most efficient and quickest way possible. Let us go back to the principle mentioned above and take it further; never be the prey, always be the predator. If the attacker has managed to put his criminal act into motion, we have to assess the situation and, if it is the case, not remain inert and passive. We must not accept the role of prey, but have to react with determination and aggressiveness, turning the psychological and tactical tables: attack the attacker. We will return to speak about this basic psychological attitude later in the book.

In the practical chapters of this book we will describe numerous shooting techniques, developed to the maximum efficiency in terms of neutralizing one or more attackers. But, even when we examine these technical aspects, we should never forget two precautions:

- Reading a book can never be a substitute for learning through hands-on courses taught by qualified and expert instructors;

- The neutralization phase, and we repeat it again, must be only the last, extreme choice and should be limited to those instances in which the threat could not be prevented, dissuaded, or avoided.

A final thought regarding prevention. As Grossman also says in *On Combat*, it is advisable to always be in Condition Yellow, always moderately alert, always aware of what is around you. When we are too distracted it is impossible to carry out even a minimum degree of protection. Our level of attention, ideally, should not fall below a certain threshold. Nevertheless, in reality every day we know how easy it is for our attention to be distracted, pressed as we are by a thousand worries and thoughts. Let us take what is probably the most important (even if not the only) sense with respect to prevention, and then, of defense: our sight. Our gaze is not constantly paying attention, it is not like a video camera that has only two options—on or off. Our gaze can be more or less alert, more or less focused, and our brain can impose a widely variable level of attention to what our gaze takes in. If each of us fixed our eyes on the same object or the same scene, it would not necessarily mean that we would all pay the same amount of attention; the degree of attention can vary from person to person and from moment to moment. We can distinguish three distinct and progressive levels of visual attention:

Seeing
Looking
Observing

Seeing is not the same as looking, and observing is taking things a step further. Let's take a simple example. We are walking along the street and, while we get ready to cross, a bus comes along. The bus passes directly in front of us while we wait on the sidewalk. We saw it. Fine; having seen the bus we avoided crossing in haste and being run over by the bus. But in addition to simply having seen the bus, did we look at it? Would we be able to say, for example, what color it was and what bus company it belonged to? Did it have advertising on its side? If we only saw it but did not look at it, then we would not be able to answer those questions. Let's go even further; was the bus full or empty? Roughly how many people were on board? Further (as an example), was the driver a man or a woman? We would be able to answer these questions only if we had observed the bus.

In order to prevent the danger of an attack, to see is essential but it is not enough. To observe is very important. And, often, observing can be a determining factor.

Try to be vigilant, alert, and reactive; this is the proper attitude for defense.

CHAPTER 3
SAFETY STANDARDS

The Israeli school is known for its attention to safety. It is a very strict school with respect to every aspect and implication of safety in handling weapons. Safety as well as combat effectiveness are two essential components of the Israeli "DNA," and it is logical that it should be so.

The Israeli shooting method, in fact, was born of the analysis and codification of the experience of decades in operational theaters, multiplied by thousands and thousands of military and civilian operators, in one of the areas of the world where it is well known that the problems of security and defense are tragically a concrete reality and an everyday occurrence. This is no abstract theory, however, but a profound focus on practical reality, considering that any mistake can have serious consequences.

The first basic premise is the safe handling of the weapon, which should come as no surprise; whatever the operator's level of technical expertise might be, use of the weapon cannot and must never ignore a perfect understanding and respect for safety standards and procedures, beginning with basic handling operations to being able to clear a jammed weapon and dealing with unforeseen problems while shooting. A failure to understand or to apply safety rules, dictated by a lack of preparation or by excessive confidence, can set off a chain of errors with very dangerous consequences for the individual, for his family members, for his training partners, and for the whole team.

The safety norms of the Israeli school are extremely precise, strict, and complete (the entire protocol includes some fifty rules that are boiled down to "only" about twenty in certain phases of basic training).

In this chapter we will examine some universal principles:

- The three basic rules of safety, that are always valid, wherever and whenever.

- The consequences of violating them (the concept of the "chain of errors").

- The two basic procedures for handling a weapon (safety checks and carrying position).

Let's look at some more detailed rules, relative to different situations or scenarios (among which we have chosen the two most common that apply to any of us, regardless of our profession or type and level of training):

> Safety rules at home
> Safety rules at the range

The Three Basic Rules

First of all, these are the three basic rules for safe weapon handling. They are "basic" in the sense that they are the foundation, the pillar on which the whole safety structure is built. We could also say that they are necessary and sufficient to avoid the most serious accidents (but in reality it is also necessary to follow other rules that we will see further along in this chapter).

For sure, violating one or more of these three rules opens the door to really tragic risks. It is therefore indispensable for us to learn these rules not only by mechanically memorizing them, but (in a manner of speaking) with our whole being, with our mind and body; we must make them part of our "muscular memory" and, at the same time, we must always keep them in mind with the utmost clarity, attention, and mental presence.

1). Always consider the weapon to be loaded and therefore dangerous.

Any weapon, be it ours or someone else's, should always and unconditionally be considered to be loaded and therefore dangerous. Until we are able to check ourselves, using the safety check procedure (which we will soon describe in this chapter), we must assume that it is loaded. Even if we are told that it is unloaded, even if it is the gun's owner who so states, and even if we ourselves say it or think we remember it as such, we must not consider it to be unloaded and thus safe until we have personally checked it.

This is a basic rule that absolutely cannot be ignored. It is very simple and has no nuances; there is no "if," no "but," no "except." When in the presence of a weapon, we should not stop to think ("Did I empty the chamber? Was the magazine inserted or not?" or "Did I see the owner unload it? But did I see it properly?" etc.) nor should we take it for granted that it is unloaded (which would be even more serious). No doubts: always take for granted that it is loaded and then check it out carefully.

Only thus can we develop an automatic approach that is marked by the highest degree of caution, avoiding superficiality or an excess of confidence that are potential precursors of tragic accidents. Remember the old adage: "Most firearms victims were killed by an empty weapon" (or so they thought).

2). Never, for any reason, point a gun at anything other than a target in a safe area.
When in your hand, the weapon should never be pointed at ourselves or at any other person, be it on the range (towards the instructor, training partners, or bystanders) or at home (family members, friends, neighbors, passersby in the street outside the window, etc.). Never, for any reason. Not as a distraction, or (even worse) as a joke.

The weapon should be held and aimed only and exclusively towards a safe area that we have expressly identified as such: at a firing range, for example, it would be the backstop in front of which the targets are set up; at home, it would be a corner that we have carefully selected and, if necessary, prepared for that specific use (as we will soon explain).

We must pay attention to where we point the weapon every moment that we are handling it, and not only at the end of a movement; in other words, we are careful where we are pointing the weapon even while we are taking it out of or replacing it in its holster or picking it up and putting it down where it is stored. The weapon, and more specifically, the muzzle has to be like an extension of our hand and we must be instinctively aware of its position and of its orientation in space.

3). Always keep your finger outside the trigger guard until the moment we decide to activate the weapon.

No gun fires by itself. A firearm is an inert piece of metal until it is taken into the hand and is cocked and loaded, and in particular until the trigger is pulled. Whatever its particular mechanical configuration might be, the weapon is made so that it will not fire until the trigger is pulled. This means that the concept of an "accidental shooting" is a forced concept and does not correspond to reality. If a gun fires it is because someone pulled the trigger.

Because of this it is fundamentally important to always keep the finger away from the trigger until the instant when one decides to intentionally pull it (whether it is to fire the weapon or to dry fire it to lower the hammer and deactivate the firing pin).

Figure 3.1: Keeping the index finger outside the trigger guard is a basic safety rule. It is valid during static handling operations (such as the safety check) as well as during more dynamic actions and during exercises under stress.

During all phases of handling the weapon (including placing it into and withdrawing it from the holster) the index finger has to absolutely remain outside the trigger guard; the ideal position is to have it extended and resting on the frame of the weapon, above the front of the trigger guard (*Figure 3.1*).

(*Attention*: not even that is an absolute guarantee, because under conditions of extreme stress or agitation the muscles of the hand could contract involuntarily and the finger could slip into contact with the trigger and pull it. This is why it is essential to follow all of the rules of safety, such as for example not to point the weapon at oneself or other innocent persons).

Accidents Are the Result of a Series of Mistakes

An accident never happens without some reason, it is not a casual isolated event that is suspended in a vacuum, so to speak. Every accident due to human factors normally is the result of a combination of circumstances and actions. Briefly, every accident is the result of a sequence of errors that are linked to each other.

This applies also and above all to accidents involving firearms. It is actually improper to call them "accidents" because they are the consequence of violating one or more safety rules (except for very rare cases of mechanical failure, but even in those cases the human element enters into play as a peripheral factor that can potentially exacerbate the situation).

The seriousness of the accident is correlated to the number of violations committed. The really tragic accidents happen when someone has violated all of the basic rules of safety. The accident springs from a chain of inexorable mistakes (violations). The three basic rules are such precisely because, if they are all followed, safety is total; if only some of them are followed (one or two), each of them however does guarantee a certain measure of safety, whereas if all of them are violated, safety drops to zero and the outcome is almost certainly fatal. Let's try to imagine the following situations:

- We have neglected to consider the weapon as loaded and dangerous, and we aimed it at someone, but at least we followed the rule of keeping our finger off the trigger; in doing so we have been guilty of taking a serious risk, but nothing irreparable has happened;

- If on the other hand we have carelessly pulled the trigger, but pointed the weapon towards a safe area, there would be a considerable scare and probably some damage, but (hopefully) no one will have been hurt;

- When does a tragedy happen? When we think the weapon is not loaded, when we aim it towards someone, and when we pull the trigger.

The violation of one rule after another leads us along a sort of pathway "through a funnel" whose outcome is inevitably a dramatic accident. Thus, we will repeat again: safety rules must always be remembered, followed, and made to be followed by others (family, friends, colleagues, training partners).

Safety Checks and How to Move a Weapon

Let's now take a look at the proper procedures to carry out a safety check, that is, to ensure that the weapon is unloaded and (if it is not) how to unload it, and to move it safely from one place to another.

Safety Check Procedures

Each time that a weapon is picked up (from where it is stored, from a briefcase, from the table, etc.) and every time that it has to be handed over to someone else or is taken from someone else, it is imperative to run a safety check. The safety check is a procedure developed to determine if the weapon is unloaded (with the magazine removed, without a round in the chamber, and with the firing pin down) so that it can be handled with complete confidence. It is a relatively simple procedure, but has to be learned perfectly, repeating it until it becomes instinctive and automatic (that notwithstanding, it should always be performed with the utmost attention and concentration).

1. Premise: Our index finger has to always be outside the trigger guard, for the entire duration of the operation, until the last possible instant (it will make contact with the trigger only and exclusively at the moment that we dry fire the weapon in order to disarm the firing pin).

2. First of all we approach the firing line (on the range) or in the safe area that has been carefully identified (at home), as we will explain in more detail shortly; no one should be in front of us, not even diagonally (*Figure 3.2*).

3. The weapon should be pointed towards the target or towards the safe area, holding it in the strong hand with the elbow level with your side so that, by simply lowering your gaze, you have a clear and complete view of the top of the slide and the ejection port.

4. Rotating the weapon and turning it upside-down (always keeping the muzzle pointed towards the target or a safe area, and without tilting it upwards or downwards), visually check to see if the magazine is inserted (*Figure 3.3*), and if it is inserted, remove it and put it aside (in a magazine pouch, in your pocket, etc.).

Figure 3.2: If you are in a group on the firing range, everyone should be lined up along the firing line to conduct the safety check.

5. Check for the absence of a magazine by touch, inserting the index or middle finger of the weak hand inside the hand grip (*Figure 3.4*). This move might seem superfluous (we have just checked visually, and maybe we have just removed the magazine) but is nevertheless still very useful; in fact, this sequence of actions has to be assimilated until it becomes automatic, so that you always do it, even under dubious circumstances (uncomfortable positions, low light conditions or absolute darkness, etc.) and/or under extreme stress, without having to stop and think. Under such conditions, it is important to double-check the status of the weapon; if we get into the habit of checking both by sight and by touch, we will be more certain of our perception and we will not risk making awkward movements and a loss of time which could be very risky in an emergency situation.

6. Once the weapon has been returned to its original position (point 3), the slide is pulled back completely using the weak hand and the inside of the weapon is looked at from above; the gaze should take in the ejection port and allow the ground beneath the weapon to be seen, as an additional proof that the magazine has been removed (*Figure 3.5*); while still keeping the slide pulled to the rear, the weapon is tilted slightly downwards and a visual check is made to verify that there is no cartridge in the chamber.

Figure 3.3: Visually check for the absence of a magazine.

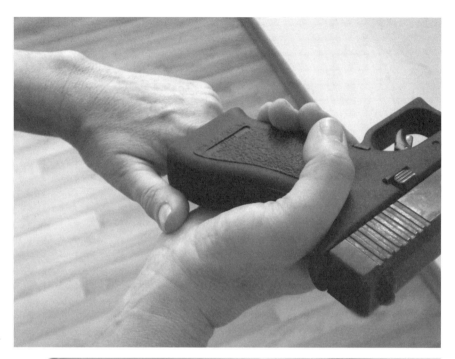

Figure 3.4: Also check for the absence of a magazine using the sense of touch by inserting a finger into the magazine well.

Figure 3.5: Visual check of the slide from above.

7. The slide is racked quickly several times (pulling the slide back to its full extent); the slide is then left in the closed positon; at this point the firing pin is active.

8. Holding the weapon pointed in a safe direction, the index finger is inserted in the trigger guard and the trigger is pulled (*Figure 3.6*); the firing pin moves forward on an empty chamber and the weapon is finally in the rest position, unloaded.

9. We are now certain that the weapon is unloaded and safe, and we can put it back in its holster or hold it in the carry position (see following). *Attention*: up until and including this moment we always have to be facing the safe position; only after having placed the weapon in its holster or having picked it up in the carry position, can we turn and move.

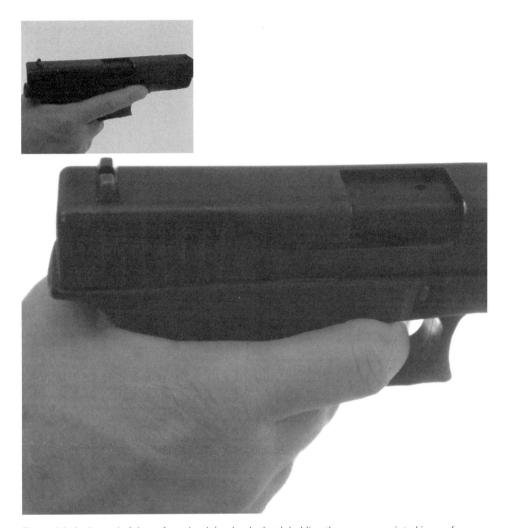

Figure 3.6: At the end of the safety check (and only then), holding the weapon pointed in a safe direction, the index finger enters the trigger guard and pulls the trigger to dry fire and bring the firing pin to the rest position.

Carry Position for the Weapon

After having carried out the safety check, if we do not return the weapon to its holster we have to grasp it securely before leaving the firing line or any time that we move from one place to another.

Figure 3.7: The "hammer" transport position.

The carry position that we use calls for grasping the weapon, once the safety check has been performed, as follows, which can be described as the "hammer" grip (*Figure 3.7*):

- Barrel pointed downwards;

- Fingers wrapped around the exterior of the barrel and the forward portion of the trigger guard;

- Pistol grip facing forward (as though it were a hammer) so that anyone standing in front of the pistol can visually note the absence of a magazine;

- If the size of the weapon and of our hand allow it, it is advisable to hold your thumb over the hammer (on top of the slide).

In this manner, the weapon's muzzle is pointed in a sufficiently safe direction (downwards), the weapon is grasped in such a way that it is impossible to cock it, and anyone nearby can see the status of the weapon and warn us in the event that we overlooked something in our safety check ("Look who has a magazine in his weapon!").

Rules for Storing and Handling a Weapon at Home

Statistics show that most accidents with legally owned firearms happen in the home or in the home environment (*Figure 3.8*).

If we think about it, in effect, there are a number of factors at the firing range that help us maintain proper concentration and avoid any mistakes. The range is well-structured and organized, subdivided into clearly identified areas that are well marked; the entrance and registration area, the shooting stations, the firing line, the backstops with the targets, the partitions dividing one station from another, and so on. In addition there is always a range officer or instructor who maintains a watchful eye, ready to take action in case of any unsafe conduct by a shooter.

At home, however, we are alone. We are in our own environment, an environment that on one hand is familiar to us (which lowers our attention threshold and which leads us to assume behavior that is often too relaxed) and on the other hand does not have the strict rules of a firing range. What is a safe direction to aim the weapon?

Figure 3.8: Domestic accidents due to mistakes and oversights while handling weapons have tragic consequences.

Who or what is behind that wall (that may be of sheetrock or of perforated building blocks and thus easily penetrated)? No one is there to observe our actions and to call us out in case of clumsy or dangerous moves. Thus, the home is a place that calls for great attention and care in storing and handling a weapon.

Let's now look at some basic security rules in sequential order with respect to common operations carried out at home; the choice of how and where to store the weapon, identifying the area in which to perform the safety check (both of these choices have a priority and preliminary character), the warnings concerning handling and carrying the weapon, and finally some words on maintenance and cleaning.

Store the Weapon Without a Round in the Chamber
and Without a Magazine Inserted

When we think of the best conditions under which to store a weapon, the concept of "best" cannot have an abstract and absolute value but has to be viewed in context. In the context of a "normal" life, in a civilian urban environment, facts show that the probability of an accident with a weapon (wounding oneself, a family member, or a neighbor) is much higher compared to the probability of an attack that requires its immediate use. It is thus reasonable to put the emphasis on the safety (of yourself and of others) in the first mentioned case, finding an appropriate compromise between safety and the availability of the weapon itself.

With an empty chamber and without a magazine the weapon is in a completely safe state (*Figure 3.9*). Thinking of an extreme home defense scenario, in case of need, to insert a magazine and chamber a round requires only a few moments; for a person whose preparedness is average, the time it takes (between the time the weapon is grasped and the moment it is pointed at the target) compared to an already loaded weapon is practically irrelevant.

Figure 3.9: Storing a weapon with an empty chamber and with the magazine removed.

That's not all. Let's try to follow the following reasoning, which we will push to the extreme on purpose, not to state it as an absolute truth but, as always, to stimulate thought. The act of inserting a magazine and chambering a round represents an action that makes us immediately certain of the status of the weapon (unloaded, loaded, ready to fire). Otherwise, is a weapon that has a magazine in it loaded or unloaded? Does it have a round in the chamber or not? Sure, now that we are awake and clear-headed we know the status, but if we were to be awakened suddenly by an attack in the middle of the night, would we be just as sure or would we spontaneously lose a few seconds to physically check the status of the weapon? And it is at that point that the theoretical advantage in terms of speed could show itself?

But most of all, as we underscore many times in the book, in our experience, we find it useful to adopt a single, consistent method without too many complications and distinctions. If we always keep an empty chamber, we know that in any given moment we only have to rack the slide and chamber a round to be ready to fire, without too many "ifs" and "buts." If, on the other hand, we were to begin to distinguish between a thousand different situations, for example if we kept the weapon without a round in the chamber during the day but with a loaded chamber at night (thinking that we would be "more ready" for an emergency), in case of need we might not be completely certain as to the weapon's status and would not be able to benefit from the automatic reactions developed during training. Briefly, by keeping the weapon with an empty chamber we maximize safe handling (a primary requirement in a civilian context) as well as simplicity and effectiveness of training: one rule, one solution.

In fact, we will say even more: in a situation such as this (being suddenly awakened in the middle of the night) it is preferable and advisable that our reaction not be too quick. It might seem paradoxical, but if we think about it, it is logical. Imagine ourselves to be barely awake, we are still half asleep and at the same time excited by adrenalin, so we are far from being completely lucid.

Having a weapon ready to fire immediately may in all probability cause us to react too quickly and reflexively, running a serious risk of shooting ourselves or some family member or guest who may have innocently caused the noise that woke and alarmed us, or who at that moment may have been in another room and gone to the bathroom, etc. Rather, in our experience, to be used to perform certain basic operations such as inserting a magazine and racking the slide to chamber a round helps us, or better yet forces us, to be aware of what we are doing and to clearly identify the threat (distinguishing between a real and a presumed threat). As we mentioned in the first chapter, according to the Israeli method, racking the slide to chamber a round is all one action along with aiming and identifying the threat.

It is obvious that, in a different context and in a high-risk condition or of hostilities in progress, it can make sense to insert the magazine (and also to chamber a round, even if in this respect the considerations presented in other parts of the book remain valid). On the other hand, if we leave home for a weekend we can leave the weapon in its gun safe, not only without its magazine, but possibly even disassembled (as in this case the need for immediate use is almost zero). In daily life it is probable that the ideal solution is a middle road between these two options.

Let's try to imagine the opposite situation; we decide to keep the weapon always with a magazine inserted and a round in the chamber. Given the remote (hopefully, very remote) chance of having to use the weapon for defense, in which there would be a relative advantage, there would be a very serious daily risk of lack of attention and accidents with potentially tragic consequences.

Let's Keep the Weapon in a Secure Place
For normal storage of the weapon we should choose the most secure place inside the home. Even in this respect, as we have just said, safety and easy access for use represent two extremes, between which we have to seek a compromise or the best balance depending on our circumstances.

A safe offers the greatest amount of security but does slow down access to the weapon. There are safes with electronic locks, using either a keypad or the owner's fingerprint identification; but what happens if the electric power fails and the backup batteries are dead? A key can be used in an emergency, but that implies that we have time to realize that the standard lock is not working and that we have time to get the key. To the contrary, keeping the weapon on the nightstand makes it readily available but significantly reduces safety in the family environment.

Let's never forget that we have an ethical and legal obligation to store our weapons with the utmost care. A loaded weapon left lying around the house, especially if children or third parties are present even occasionally, represents a serious physical, moral, and legal risk. It may seem trivial to say it again, but we should never lower our vigilance. Nothing is easier, for example, for anyone who habitually carries a weapon to give in to very dangerous "laziness" and when returning home to limit himself to putting the weapon somewhere close at hand without taking the proper safety precautions. The problems are lurking just around the corner.

In the Presence of Children,
Let Us Make Sure That the Weapon Is Not Within Their Reach

Even this may seem an obvious and trivial rule, but it is far from it. All of the rules regarding safe storage of the weapon at home should be adopted based on the context and presence of other people in the house, in particular, and most of all if there are children there. Children have an innate sense of curiosity and have no knowledge of a real weapon and of the danger it poses; it is a mix of high-risk factors. It is therefore imperative to make sure that the weapon is placed somewhere that is out of their reach. That is the general rule, but it is not enough.

What "children" are we speaking of? We have to realize that a four-year old is one thing, while a young boy of eleven or twelve is another. Their psychophysical characteristics are different, their capabilities differ and therefore the type and degree of risk differ.

Not only is their strength and manual dexterity different, so that it would be very difficult for a very young child to pull rack the slide on a semiautomatic pistol that did not already have a round in the chamber (attention: we said difficult, but not impossible, so don't take it for granted!) while a somewhat older child can do it without much difficulty; their "range of action" is also different. If we are dealing with a four-year-old child, for example, the weapon can be considered to be sufficiently safe (even if not optimally) stored at the top of a high closet which the child cannot climb (even with the aid of a chair) or in a drawer locked with a key (the key should be kept in another room). But if we are dealing with a twelve-year-old child such measures do not provide an effective safeguard. Young children have an extraordinary capacity for exploring every nook and cranny of a house, they are imaginative and persistent, and their intelligence makes them capable of uncovering and overcoming many obstacles which adults, mistakenly, feel are a barrier to children. It is in their nature.

So, if there are children in the home, it is imperative to store the weapon in a condition and in a place that makes it inaccessible to them, finding the right solution based on the situation, the environment, the layout of the house, the number and type of weapons present (which can call for different methods of storage), and the characteristics of those children.

As always, also in this case we are not dealing with a pre-packaged solution, but are recommending clear-mindedness, awareness, and an accurate assessment of the actual circumstances.

Let Us Establish a Safe Area in Which to Carry Out the Safety Check

As we have said, our home can induce a false sense of safety and confidence. It is important to act scrupulously for taking care of our weapon at home, and that we make a series of decisions at the outset. One of the first decisions to make carefully has to do with a safe area in which we can check our weapon. Where can we point the weapon so as to exclude any risk stemming from an accidental discharge?

We cannot point the weapon towards the ceiling, the floor, or a wall on the other side of which there may be a person. It is obvious that we have to stay away from doors and windows. We also have to avoid very hard surfaces that could cause dangerous and uncontrollable ricochets.

Figure 3.10: Vases or bags full of sand or dirt can help us to set up a safe area to check our weapons in our home.

Let us then choose a place that has none of these risk factors, and which also has a container, a surface, or some type of material able to absorb any accidental discharge (things that are already present in the environment or purposely placed there), for example, a flower pot or a vase full of dirt placed in a corner of the room; a corner with something stuffed or soft (pillows, magazines, phone books, bags full of rags, paper, or sand); if in the garden, a bucket full of water or dirt, and so on (*Figure 3.10*).

We Should Always Consider the Weapon to Be Loaded and Therefore Dangerous

It is the first rule of safety, which we underlined at the beginning of the chapter; every weapon should always be considered to be loaded and thus potentially dangerous. We refer you back to the previous pages for a review of this rule that cannot be ignored. It is a rule that also and most of all applies within the walls of our home, where it is easier to underestimate risks and to make serious mistakes, and where unfortunately accidents happen with a significantly high statistical frequency. Our weapon is always a weapon, a potentially lethal object. We have to know it, respect it, and use it with the caution it is due. Always.

Each Time We Pick Up or Lay Down the Weapon We Must Carry Out a Safety Check

We have previously seen the correct procedure for performing a safety check on a weapon. Each time that we take the weapon from its storage space, and each time that we put it back, we have to perform a safety check. It is only by doing this that we can be certain that the weapon is in the status that you want (that is, as we have discussed above, with no magazine and with an empty chamber).

When We Have to Move Our Weapon We Must Use the Proper Carry Method

Let's imagine that we have just performed our safety check; now we have to carry the weapon somewhere else (to another room, to clean it, or to put it in a gun case to bring it to the range, etc.). The weapon should be in the safest condition possible, and not ready for immediate use. We will therefore use the position that we described previously; grasp the weapon in a "hammer" position, with the muzzle pointing downward and the grip facing forward, with the fingers wrapped around the frame without entering the trigger guard.

When We Put the Weapon in Its Holster, the Thumb of the Grasping Hand Has to Rest on the Hammer (or on the Rear of the Slide)

When the weapon is inserted into the holster, it is easy for friction to rack the slide far back enough to chamber a round, arm the hammer, and make the pistol ready to fire. We would then find ourselves in a risky condition for our safety and that of others, not being aware of the weapon's status.

To avoid this risk, you only have to get into the habit of always keeping your thumb resting on the hammer (or on the rear of the slide for weapons lacking an exposed hammer) so as to hold the slide in a fixed position while the weapon is slid into the holster (*Figure 3.11*).

This is a habit that we recommend be assimilated and rendered automatic because it is a rule that always applies, regardless of the mechanical layout of one weapon compared to another. Historically, this rule was developed when the vast majority of Israeli operational personnel adopted the FN Browning HP pistol (*Figure 3.12*); it had a half-cock hammer safety that could be activated by a very short backward movement of the slide (barely a fraction of an inch). With the hammer at half cock, the manual safety could also be engaged (the safety catch sprang into the slot in the slide) by the same involuntary movement.

While inserting the weapon into the holster without holding the thumb on the hammer, it was very easy for friction or some type of snag to produce this result, whose implications were potentially very serious; when the weapon was drawn the operator would have found himself with the weapon with the safety on, without expecting it, with consequences that can easily be imagined. For this reason, during training, the rule of the thumb on the hammer while inserting the weapon into the holster was introduced.

The rule is still completely applicable today even while using different weapons. In fact, this rule does not have any disadvantages (it thus costs nothing, so to speak) and can offer only an advantage,

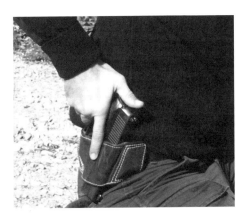

Figure 3.11: When inserting the weapon into its holster it is advisable to keep your thumb on the hammer.

Figure 3.12: The Browning HP (High Power) semiautomatic pistol: the manual safety catch is shown in the circle.

or in the worst case, can be "another thing" that does no harm. It should be underlined that for many weapons currently in service this rule shows its worth, even for pistols without an exposed hammer such as the Glock (and all similar semi-double action or equivalent pistols); with these pistols only a slight rearward movement of the slide is enough to activate the firing pin, and the absence of an exposed hammer makes the weapon's status harder to determine.

Thus, recapping, this is a rule that has a historical origin but which is still valid today. By adopting this automatic procedure we will be ready to handle any weapon safely, be it from the past, a current weapon, or something in the future.

Let Us Be Fully Knowledgeable About Our Weapon and Its Parts

It behooves us to be fully knowledgeable about our weapon; to know its characteristics, its mechanical components, and its method of functioning. It is important to master the weapon and to know how to handle it in complete safety. We have to know how to disassemble and reassemble it at least so that we can clean it and perform basic maintenance. In addition to being indispensable, these operations also help in acquiring a growing familiarity with the mechanics of the weapon and to keep an eye on the proper working order of each component. To know your weapon well also means that you are able to deal with any problems, irregularities, or jams with due speed and competence.

While Cleaning the Weapon,
There Should Be No Ammunition Nearby

While cleaning the weapon, be it on a desk, a table, or a workbench, no ammunition should be nearby. A safety check should be performed before beginning to clean the weapon and the magazine has been removed, which if loaded, should be left in the storage area or in another room (naturally, even the magazine should be cleaned, as long as it is completely empty). While cleaning, not even a single cartridge should be anywhere near the weapon.

Distraction is always lying in wait. It can happen, for example, that during assembly, disassembly, or cleaning, we become curious and, to check on the condition of the chamber, if we have some ammunition handy, we grab a round and insert it manually into the chamber. The phone rings, or our spouse calls us, or one of the children gets hurt and we leave or otherwise have our attention compromised. Then we return to the weapon, we assemble it and, without thinking, have left a round in the chamber. It may seem like a forced example, but it is absolutely real, and it is in

Figure 3.13: While cleaning the weapon, keeping ammunition nearby is forbidden.

such cases that accidents, even dramatic ones, can happen. We could cite many similar examples.

In brief: during maintenance of the weapon there is no need for ammunition, other than to expose us to unnecessary risk. So, let's leave the ammunition elsewhere (*Figure 3.13*).

Rules for Handling a Weapon on the Range

The firing range represents a different environment than that of the home; rules of behavior are clearly indicated and there are supervisory personnel such as range officers and instructors who help us to follow the safety regulations. But even in that context, when we are together with other people (instructors, training partners) just as when we are alone and no one is supervising us, we must pay the utmost attention and never let down our guard. Safety rules are always applicable, without exception.

We Should Always Consider the Weapon to Be Loaded and Therefore Dangerous

We have already mentioned it several times but we will repeat it again: this is the first rule of safety. Every weapon should be considered to be loaded and dangerous. We have commented at length on this subject at the beginning of the chapter. We will limit ourselves here just to mention it, because it is always a valid rule, even at a firing range.

Rules may differ from one range to another, especially those for dynamic shooting, where there may be different standards depending on the type of course and the instructor's school of origin. Some are used to working with a round in the chamber while others are not, and others leave room for a certain variety of situations (sometimes with a round in the chamber and sometimes not, based on different scenarios and exercises). We have no doubts and, as we have already said, we always work with an empty chamber, but we cannot be sure beforehand of the status of the weapon belonging to whoever is in the firing lane next to us and who comes to train alongside us.

In any case, it is not a question of observation or of reasoning, as the rule is absolute: we always have to consider every weapon to be loaded and thus dangerous until we run a safety check on it.

Never Point the Weapon, For Any Reason, Towards Ourselves, Our Training Partners, or the Instructor

This rule has also been discussed at the beginning of the chapter, but we will repeat it here. When it is grasped, the weapon must never be aimed, under any circumstances or for any reason, towards ourselves or other persons; the instructor, our training partners, or bystanders.

While we are not practice firing, the weapon should be on a table or in its holster. During the shooting practice, the weapon is aimed only at the target or a properly identified safe area, as defined by the following rule.

The Unholstered Weapon Is Aimed Only Towards a Safe Area

Inside the range itself, an area that is safe towards which weapons can be pointed while performing a safety check should be identified and clearly pointed out to everyone taking part in the training (*Figure 3.14*). Normally it is a backstop along which the targets are aligned, and which consists of a substance that can absorb bullets with no risk of ricochet (bullet traps, sand, earth).

Figure 3.14: The safe area, towards which you should point your weapon while checking it, should be clearly and unmistakably identified. It is usually the backstop against which the targets are lined up.

For certain exercises, there could also be targets off to the side of the range; in this case as well, however, the safety zone is limited to the backstop, and at the end of the exercise (even though we may have fired at one of the side targets last) we should turn again towards the backstop before performing our safety check.

We Always Perform a Safety Check at the Beginning and End of Each Shooting Session

Before and after every shooting session we step up to the firing line, turn towards the safety area (see above), and we carry out our safety check. Only by systematically following this rule can we be certain of maintaining the highest level of safety. At the end of the firing session, in particular, by performing the safety check, we can ensure that we are inserting a weapon with an empty chamber and without a magazine into its holster (this is the status in which we have to carry our weapon between one session and the next, as we have already explained above).

The Safety Check Is Performed on the Firing Line

In order to carry out a safety check, we always have to take a position on the firing line and turn towards the safe area, as we have repeated many times. If there is more than one of us, we have to make sure that we are all properly aligned and that whoever is not performing their safety check is behind us; there should be no one in front of us, not even off to the side. Be aware, for example, that no one approaches the targets along the backstop to change the targets while we are busy performing the safety check; this is a very dangerous distraction.

It is important to follow this rule and to maintain order on the firing range; the confusion that at times can be seen in certain circumstances is to be absolutely avoided, with people checking weapons outside of the firing line, perhaps under a roof and around a table, someone pointing in one direction and someone else in another, mixed in with people who are chatting or who are smoking, and so on. Never lower your threshold of attention and never give in to such chaotic situations, which are as unacceptable as they are risky (*Figure 3.15*).

Figure 3.15: The safety check and the general handling of weapons should never be done outside the firing line. At the table and under the roof no one should ever pull out and handle a weapon while other people are busy and distracted by other activities.

When We Move the Weapon from or to the Firing Line, Use the Correct Carry Position

Even at the range, when we handle our weapon outside of the firing line, we always and under all circumstances must adopt the safe method of carrying the weapon which we described at the beginning of the chapter; the "hammer" position with the muzzle pointing downward and the grip forward (*Figures 3.2* and *3.7*). Only on the firing line can we grasp the weapon by its grip (holding the muzzle pointed towards the safe area and the index finger away from the trigger).

When We Place the Weapon in Its Holster the Thumb
of the Hand Grasping It Must Rest on the Hammer
(or on the Rear of the Slide)

This rule has also been described, but it is worthwhile mentioning it here. When inserting the gun in its holster, the thumb must always be resting on the hammer (or on the rear of the slide on pistols without an exposed hammer); that way we are sure that the slide does not move while we slip the gun into the holster. If we do not take that precaution, there is a risk that the slide, moving to the rear, inadvertently arms the weapon or activates the firing pin (for weapons without a hammer) and that we find ourselves with a weapon that is in a status other than we believe. In the preceding pages we explained both the historical reason for the development of this rule, as well as the reasons why it is still a valid rule.

It Is Important to Know the Exercise Area
and to Check Its Security

Prior to a firing session, when we arrive at a range we need to examine it scrupulously (especially if it is not our normal firing range) to make sure of its safety status.

The range should have a proper layout. The target line should be properly identified. The area should be completely isolated and protected with respect to the adjacent properties by means of earthen berms or other inert and non-solid material (to avoid ricochets) of adequate thickness (to prevent bullets from passing through) and height (at least ten feet). The backstop should be dirt or sand or of other material capable of absorbing rounds without any fear of ricochet of bullets or fragments (for example, backstops should not be made of stones or other hard materials). The ground itself should not be slippery and should be as consistent as possible (dirt, grass) and without any obstacles or hard objects (such as medium to large-size stones) off of which bullets could ricochet.

We should take care to properly position the target supports and to keep the area free of all useless and potentially dangerous items, placing them off to the side or behind us.

CHAPTER 4

GRASPING AND DRAWING THE WEAPON

With this chapter we will begin a discussion of technical and practical subjects. Although we may not always repeat it, the warning that in the first place every rule and every technique represent basic principles (which in reality can have variations, exceptions, and be subject to modification) and that, in the second place, the explanations provided in this book can never fully replace hands-on learning under the guidance of a qualified instructor, is always applicable.

Note: From this point forward, in the description of each of the techniques, we assume that the shooter is right-handed, that is, that the strong (dominant) hand that grasps the pistol is the right hand. It is obvious that a left-handed shooter has to perform the movements in inverse order.

How to Hold the Pistol and Pull the Trigger
Under normal conditions the pistol is grasped with both hands.

The pistol should be grasped by the strong hand so that it is aligned with the forearm, as its ideal extension (*Figure 4.1*). This results in a solid grip and instinctive aiming. The pistol hilt (the upper part of the pistol grip) is grasped between the thumb and index finger. If the axis of the pistol is not aligned with the forearm, there will most likely be problems with aiming and controlling the weapon (*Figure 4.2*).

The strong hand wraps around the pistol grip and the index finger rests on the frame, outside and above the trigger guard, until it is time to fire (as we have explained when discussing safety rules).

The weak hand wraps around the strong hand; the fingers are underneath the trigger guard (and not around it, even in the case of trigger guards with a "combat" silhouette and checkering); the thumb rests over the thumb of the right hand (*Figure 4.3*).

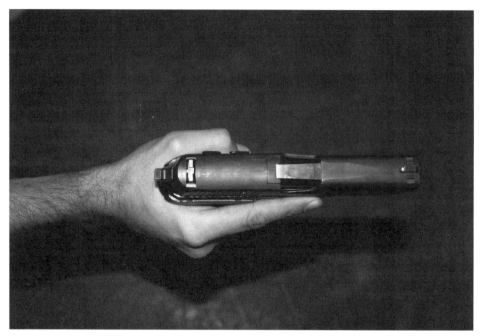

Figure 4.1: The pistol should be held as though it were an extension of your limb: grasped by the strong hand, aligned with your forearm both horizontally as well as vertically.

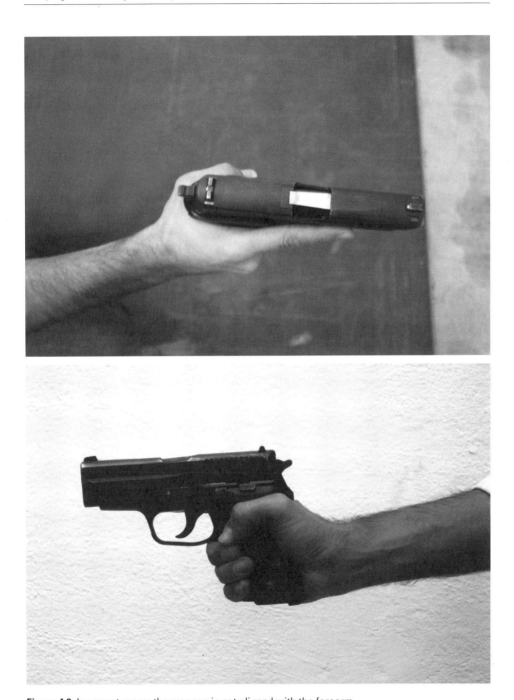

Figure 4.2: Incorrect grasp: the weapon is not aligned with the forearm.

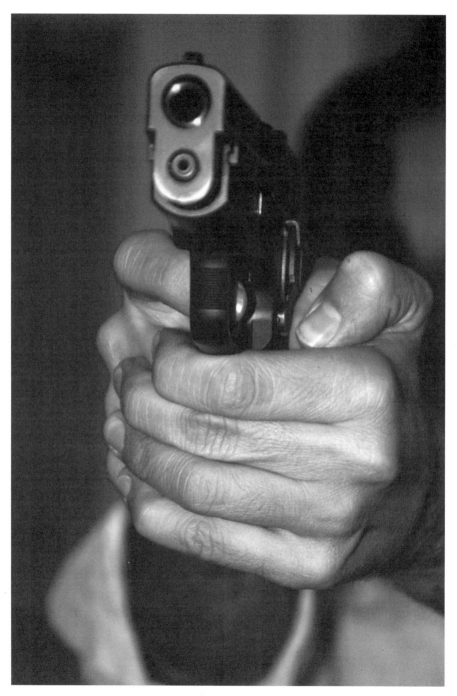

Figure 4.3: The weak hand wraps around the strong hand
(and not the front of the trigger guard).

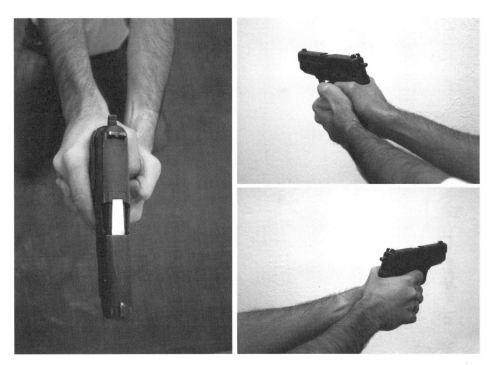

Figure 4.4: The pistol is grasped with both hands, as though in a vise, with the thumbs closed over each other.

The thumbs of both hands are bent and closed (not extended) so that the weapon is grasped firmly, as in a vise (*Figure 4.4*).

The shooter's entire body, basically, is turned frontally towards the target (*Figure 4.5*). The legs are spread, flexed, and under tension. It is a position that, not by chance, we have already defined as the "combat" position, not simply as the "shooting" position. Both arms are extended completely forward, and the pistol is thus aligned in the center (with respect to the axis of the body) so that the line of sight (rear sight and front sight axis) is at eye level. We will shortly analyze the use of the view and of the sight components.

Under certain conditions the pistol can be grasped by only one hand (usually the strong hand, but in emergency situations it could be the weak hand), for example when the threat is unexpected and too close and there is no time to assume the standard two-handed stance.

Figure 4.5: Two-handed combat firing position.

Figure 4.6: One-handed combat firing position.

In such an instance, the basic rules discussed above apply; weapon-forearm alignment, hand wrapped around the weapon, thumb bent and firmly on the pistol grip, arm extended towards the target.

The other hand could be unusable because of a wound or because it is restricted or otherwise engaged (in carrying an object, in holding, protecting, or moving a person). If, however, it is free the Israeli school teaches that it should be extended forward and to the side, towards the outside of the body (*Figure 4.6*).

There are many purposes for this position: it gives stability to the body, it maintains a dynamic balance, it protects us from being pushed or attacked, it keeps the weak arm and hand ready to support the pistol as a follow-on move, and so on. Remember that we are always thinking of real-life defense scenarios, or of "dirty" and chaotic events with people, obstacles, and unexpected situations of all types, rather than the orderly and sterile environment of the firing range.

We would like to add a few notes and underscore some aspects regarding the use of the fingers (thumb and index). It is important for the thumbs to be folded as when closing a fist and closed around the pistol's grip, precisely because, as we have just seen, we are not speaking of target shooting but of operational defense shooting. Tightening and closing the thumbs is consistent both with instinct, which causes us to contract our muscles and close our hands as a protective reaction to a threat, as well as with real defense requirements. With the thumbs closed it is much easier to hold the weapon tightly in your hand or, in more technical terms, to guarantee that the weapon is securely held, against the risk that it could slip out of our hand following some sort of impact (from people who are fleeing, bump into us, grab hold of us, etc.) or, even worse, that it is yanked from our hand by an attacker. This type of grasp is even more useful when firing with one hand, and in case of need, also allows the weapon to be used as a non-firing means of defense, to use it as a club against the attacker when we have run out of ammunition, if the gun is jammed, or when the distance and the speed of the attack do not allow us to reload. Even in a case in which we have our weapon in hand but our assessment of the type of threat does not call for shooting, we can use the weapon in this manner and it is important to grasp it tightly as we have described.

Do a test. Take an empty weapon (always perform a safety check) and grasp it with both hands keeping the thumbs extended forward, parallel to the pistol's frame. Then ask a friend to pull it from you by grabbing the barrel and slide by lifting it

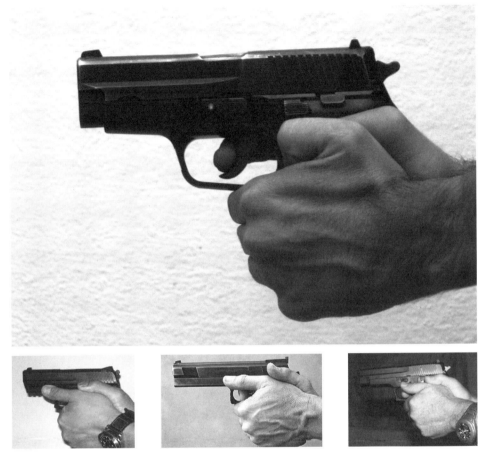

Figure 4.7: For defense and operational shooting, a grip using tightly closed thumbs is preferable (large upper photo); rather than keeping them extended along the frame (smaller photos below).

upward or to the side. You will immediately feel that your grasp is not strong enough. Then try grasping the pistol with your thumbs closed tight and repeat the operation; you will easily become aware of the difference. You can actually carry out this experiment on your own, grasping the weapon with only one hand and trying to grab and move it with the other. When the thumb is closed like a fist, the grip is much more solid. Therefore, also in this respect, from our point-of-view, instinct, science, and operational experience all provide similar evidence (*Figure 4.7*).

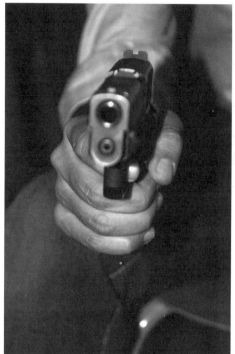 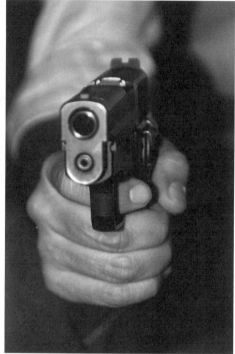

Figure 4.8: Only the tip of the index finger should rest on the trigger (photo on the left). If the index finger is inserted too far into the trigger guard and wraps around the trigger too much (photo on the right) trigger pull will not be very accurate and shots will be jerky and erratic.

Finally, but certainly not least important, we will speak in detail about the use of the index finger of the firing hand. When the trigger finger is brought to the trigger to fire, the movement should not be too sharp or excessive. Only the tip, or the ball, of the index finger should contact the trigger. Thus, neither too little nor too much of the index finger should be inserted into the trigger guard; if the finger goes too far into the trigger guard, pulling the trigger with the middle segment of the finger, the proper contact will not be made and the shots will be subject to jerking and inaccuracy. Briefly: the hand has to grasp the weapon tightly, but the index finger itself has to have a relatively "light" touch on the trigger (*Figure 4.8*).

In addition, once the index finger has taken position in the trigger guard to fire, it must always remain in contact with the trigger, shot after shot, until the shooting engagement is over. After a round has been fired, if firing is to continue, the finger should not be taken off the trigger, otherwise in the excitement of firing the next round, the finger will pull the trigger with too much force, shaking the weapon and compromising accuracy.

Not only that: it is not enough for the finger to remain in contact with the trigger, but it also has to acquire a certain degree of sensitivity and precision to manage the so-called reset. When a round is fired, the finger remains firmly fixed on the trigger while it moves to the rear, during a sequence as follows: pre-firing (the trigger moves from the rest position to the point that it stiffens immediately prior to firing); firing (the round is fired); post-firing travel (the trigger can continue its rearward movement slightly until the limit of its travel). Then the trigger is allowed to return to the forward position, with the finger always in contact. In order to truly master this shooting technique, the trigger should not be allowed to return completely forward to the rest position, but should stop its movement as soon as the reset or "click" of the firing pin is felt. This "click" happens roughly halfway through the trigger return (but the exact timing depends on the type of weapon). At that point we are ready to fire the next round. By thus controlling and limiting the forward and rearward trigger travel, greater accuracy is guaranteed (less shaking) as well as a higher rate of fire. In the hands of a trained shooter, this mastery can enable a semiautomatic weapon to be fired at a rate that makes it seem like a fully automatic weapon. The ability to quickly fire off rounds while keeping the target aligned can be a key factor in a firefight (in reality, there is no "silver bullet" and we should not fool ourselves into thinking that it is always possible to neutralize a deadly threat with a single shot).

Pointed Fire, Open Eyes, and Dominant Eye

Defense-operational shooting is essentially pointed fire, not aimed fire (except in special circumstances). Defensive reaction does not allow the time or the relaxation necessary to take accurate aim as in target shooting. In addition, the stress from sudden danger typically causes changes of visual perception.

On the one hand, your gaze tends to focus on the threat, with wide-open eyes both staring and looking directly at the target. On the other hand the so-called "tunnel effect" can manifest itself in which the vision focuses very narrowly on one aspect of the threat itself—for example, on the weapon being held by the attacker. In other words, stress and fear can induce two potentially opposing reactions; on the one hand the need to keep the field of vision as broad as possible (two wide-open eyes), and on the other hand an extreme contraction of sight that concentrates only on a very narrow focal point.

For all of these reasons, along with the need for rapid reaction, defensive shooting is done with both eyes open and turned towards the threat; we have to visually take in as much of the scene as possible (considering that in the event of a real attack we cannot be sure that, in addition to the attacker that we see, there may not be other attackers or other complicating factors) while at the same time we have to fight the tunnel effect (which, if we were to close one eye to take aim, would be drastically aggravated). Among other things, having both eyes open guarantees not only a wider field of vision but also of depth, that is, three-dimensionality and distance perception. Therefore the first rule, suggested by scientific studies on combat stress as well as by operational experience in defense shooting, is shoot with both eyes open (*Figure 4.9*).

A second point has to do with focusing your gaze: what should be brought into focus? The sight components (and which ones, the rear sight notch or the front sight blade?) or the target? There are those who maintain that you should bring the front sight into focus, while leaving both the rear sight notch and the target partly out of

Figure 4.9: Both eyes are open during defensive firing.

focus; that way, so they say, it is possible to take aim with a good degree of accuracy. Field experience by Israeli operators instead supports the choice of putting the target, that is, the attacker or threat, into focus, maintaining an overall view of the entire field of vision (*Figure 4.10*). This is an Israeli-style "cultural approach," which comes closer to being a combatant than just a shooter.

To put the front sight into focus is all very well for precision shooting, when reaction speed is not a priority or vital consideration, or when there is a great distance from the threat and the shooting has to be more accurate. But let's try to imagine a real situation of close-in danger, with an attacker who has a weapon aimed at us, on the street, in our front yard, or inside our home with all of the emotion, anxiety, poor lighting, and with the agitation that all of that brings. Let's imagine the tension and the speed with which we would try to draw our pistol and react to the looming threat. Is it really plausible that after we have drawn and pointed our pistol, while the attacker is moving and possibly even other people (passersby, neighbors, or

Figure 4.10: The focus is on the target, not on the sights.

family members) around us are moving that we can afford the time to close one eye to take aim and hit a specific part of the target? Real-life experience teaches us that it is very difficult; even if we want to, we rarely succeed. Our eyes remain wide open and fixed on the attacker, and the pistol goes where the eye goes. Above all, it is not only a question of time but also of the completeness of perception of the overall situation, of all of the danger factors and of possible unexpected developments.

Analyzing the techniques in their real-life application context and studying a great number of actual cases, it has been assessed that putting the front sight into focus carries too high a price in terms of reduced perception of the threat and of the surrounding environment; there is a significant lowering of the probability of seeing movements, or of important or even crucial changes, of the attacker or of the overall situation. On the other hand, keeping the target in focus affords us an optimal "visual compromise" for perception of the overall situation. Instinctiveness and immediacy of action are thus enhanced (as it is spontaneous to cast your glance towards the threat) as is effectiveness (as most of the visual field is kept in view).

Under these conditions, pointing the weapon is accurate if the movements and positions have been correctly assimilated during training. Our body itself helps us if we know what to do. Let's try to give a simple example. If, faced with an unexpected danger, instead of a weapon, we were to point our finger towards the threat to point out where it was, upon what would we focus our gaze? On our finger or on the threat? Obviously on the threat. And, if we were to check, we would realize that our finger points to the threat with great accuracy. This phenomenon is true not only in a situation of danger—we can point at any object, under conditions of normal daily life, and the result will always be the same. We never have to look at our finger to point to something with precision. The same is true for our pistol if we have learned how to grasp, draw, and point it properly (in the preceding pages we have stressed how important it is for the weapon to act as a sort of spontaneous extension of the arm).

The subject of the so-called "dominant eye" deserves its own separate discussion.

Even when we look with both eyes open, normally each of us has one eye that is dominant (not necessarily the right eye for right-handed people or the left for left-handers); it is the eye that assumes the priority role in vision, even though we may be unaware of it, and it is the one that we use instinctively to aim with in classical target shooting. In order to discover which eye is our dominant eye we can take a simple test: keeping both eyes open we point our weapon towards the target (making

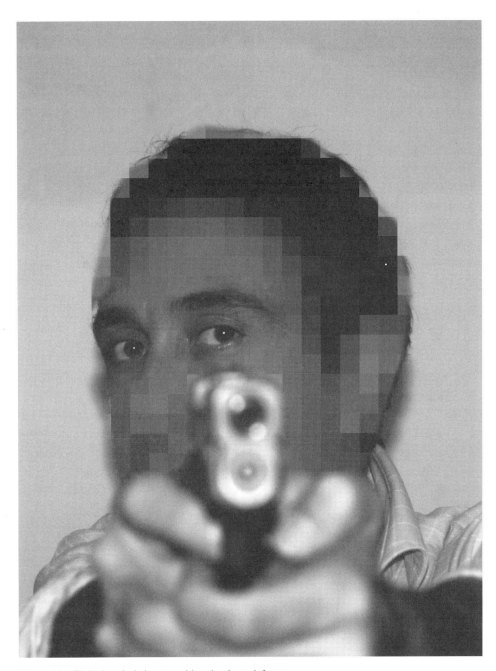

Figure 4.11: Right-handed shooter with a dominant left eye.

sure that it is unloaded, after having performed a safety check), then we alternately close our right eye and then our left eye. Only one of the two eyes will be correctly aligned along the rear sight notch, sight blade, and target (the other eye will be slightly off-center). That is our dominant eye.

Figure 4.12: If the target is at some distance and the situation allows it, you can take an instant to take aim by closing one eye for greater accuracy (but after that both eyes should again be open).

When we point and shoot, keeping both eyes open, in reality our head does not look perfectly to the front and is not symmetrically aligned with respect to the weapon, because it automatically tends to favor the position of the dominant eye. If we are right-handed and our right eye is dominant, this phenomenon is almost imperceptible or is negligible. But if we are right-handed and our left eye is the dominant eye, our head will assume a less natural position (*Figure 4.11*). The same applies if our right eye is dominant but is injured or cannot be used temporarily (because of dust, splinters, scratches, sweat, etc.). Not only that—in case of need or for reasons of operational comfort we can train the other eye to the point that it becomes the dominant eye. There are specific exercises available to achieve that result.

In summary, defensive shooting is instinctive shooting, and is done with both eyes open (pointed shooting, not aimed shooting). Only in exceptional cases , when there is a significant distance to the target and if reaction time allows it, more careful aim can be taken, briefly closing one eye to align the sights on the target (*Figure 4.12*). But both eyes must be opened again as quickly as possible, ready to take in everything relating to the attacker and everything that is taking place in the area of the engagement.

How to Draw the Pistol and Chamber a Round

Let's now look at the basic technique for drawing and arming the weapon. For clarity and ease of presentation, let's consider a very simple situation, in which the threat presents itself to our front, and we are standing, with our hands free and our pistol readily accessible. For purposes of explanation, we will break the action down into a precise sequence of phases, even though obviously in reality everything would happen seamlessly, very quickly, and without any "geometric" or artificial separations between one movement and the next:

1. Let's begin from a normal standing rest position: Facing the target, legs straight (no tension) and close to each other, shoulders relaxed, arms hanging alongside the body. The pistol, as we have mentioned in the preceding chapters, is in a belt holster on the strong (right) side, with a magazine inserted but without a round in the chamber.

Figure 4.13: The hands are positioned ready to draw.

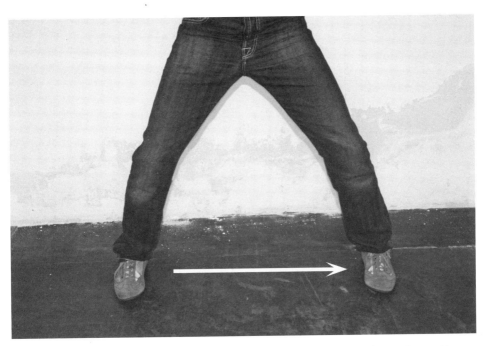

Figure 4.14: The legs are spread (the left leg is positioned forward) assuming the combat position.

2. As soon as we see the threat, we make two simultaneous movements, one with our arms and one with our legs. Arms: The right hand is positioned over the holster, sliding across the bust, open and ready to grasp the weapon; at the same time, the left hand rises and stops in front of the chest, roughly at the height of the sternum (*Figure 4.13*). Legs: The left leg shifts outwards (that is, it moves to the left), the weight remains in the center, and the legs are flexed and spread, with the feet parallel and facing forward (*Figure 4.14*). What is the reason for these initial moves? That can be quickly explained. The right hand has to become accustomed to sliding across the bust so that if we are wearing a jacket this automatic movement would cause us to unconsciously open the fold of the jacket, and we avoid the risk of any type of impact or entanglement. The left hand is preparing to grasp the weapon to chamber a round, as we shall see in a moment. The legs assume what we have defined as the "combat position" rather than just a firing position, full of dynamic tension and assuming a solid stance while at the same time ready for quick movement.

Figure 4.15: The right hand travels along the side and grabs the pistol grip. Be careful in this phase to grasp the weapon correctly (aligning the weapon with your forearm) and keep the index finger outside the trigger guard.

The left leg rather than the right is moved (except for unique cases in which circumstances would prevent it) as this would not hinder drawing the weapon, which is on the opposite side.

3. The right hand is lowered while continuing to slide along our side until it grasps the pistol grip. The first area to come into contact is the hollow between the thumb and the index finger, then the fingers wrap around the grip. During this phase the correct alignment between the weapon and the forearm is established. The index finger should rest well extended on the slide, outside the trigger guard (*Figure 4.15*).

4. The right hand extracts the pistol from its holster, and drawing it close to the body and with the index finger strictly outside the trigger guard, brings it up

Figure 4.16: The pistol is grasped with both hands and we are ready to rack the slide to chamber a round.

in front of us, roughly level with our throat (or a bit higher than chest level, bringing it as close as possible to our line of sight). During the draw the pistol barrel should remain pointed downward (during the vertical move as the weapon leaves the holster) and then is pointed forward towards the target. When the pistol is in front of us, it has to be rotated horizontally as though it were "laid down" on its side; in other words, the back of the right hand that grasps it is on top and the palm is on the bottom. At the same time, the left hand (which was positioned in front of the chest) grabs the rear of the slide and grasps the slide serrations between the thumb and index finger. At this point we find ourselves in the position illustrated in *Figure 4.16*.

5. Now we rack the slide to chamber a round. The slide is racked while facing forward, always keeping our eyes fixed on the threat; our gaze should never

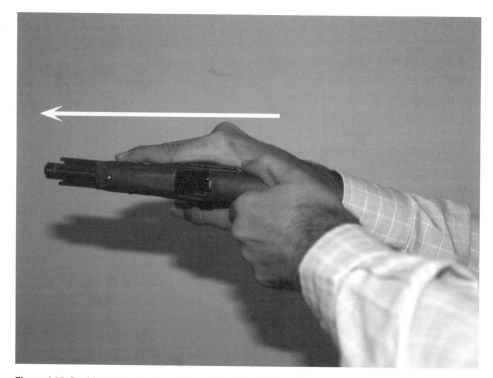

Figure 4.17: Position of the hands while racking. The left hand stays still, firmly grasping the slide. The right hand forcefully pushes the pistol forward towards the target.

be lowered towards our weapon or our hands, not even for an instant. It should be as though we are pointing to the threat with our finger (see above). In order to rack the slide properly, the left hand remains stationary, holding the slide firmly, while the right hand pushes forward (*Figure 4.17*) by forcefully extending the arm, as though we wanted to strike and punch through the target itself. As it pushes forward, the right hand makes a half-right turn so that at the end of the movement the pistol is grasped in a straight (vertical) position. It is important for the right hand to push the weapon forward and not for the left hand to pull back on the slide for two reasons. First, more force is exerted and the risk is avoided, under stress, of not pulling the slide far enough back to properly arm the pistol. As an aside, this is the same technique that is used to clear some types of jams, as we shall see later in the book. Second, the forward movement of the hand that grasps the pistol is part of lining up on the target (so much so that in the Hebrew language this movement is defined as "to rack/ to point"). We have already spoken at length of the reasons why the Israeli school prefers to work with an empty chamber, in terms of absolute priority for safety, but we would add a few practical observations here regarding this action of racking. The time required for the movement is minimal, barely a fraction of a second more compared to someone who draws and points a weapon that has a round already in the chamber. But this very minimum time lag, far from representing a simple disadvantage (it would be so only on paper, or on a stopwatch, but as we have said the reality of armed defense is somewhat more complex), rather enables better accuracy in identifying the target and deciding whether to shoot or not. In addition, it can happen that in the heat of the moment, while drawing, the right hand may grasp the weapon incorrectly; fine, when the left hand grasps the slide, in case of need it allows the right hand to be quickly repositioned properly on the pistol grip.

6. As soon as the right arm has been extended pointing the weapon at the target, the left hand moves to join the right hand, assuming the standard two-handed grasp that we described at the beginning of the chapter (*Figure 4.5*). Now we are ready to open fire against the threat.

The Hidden Draw (Clothing)

In reality, naturally, it is rare that extracting a weapon can be performed under optimal conditions; there can be a thousand unexpected situations, surprises, obstacles, distractions, and physical and mechanical problems. In this book we cannot examine every possible variation; on the one hand, it is obvious, because it is a potentially inexhaustible subject, while on the other hand, because of our precise (and previously declared) intention to keep an open mind, rather than to get into an illusory list of petty rules and specific cases. The point, as always, is to assimilate the essence of technique and then be ready to face the unexpected at any moment.

Nevertheless, there are certain "obstacles" which are daily occurrences and which can be considered in advance, such as our clothing, which changes according to our circumstances and to the season. Quite often, while we train on the firing range we do so wearing ad hoc clothing, worn purposely to ease our movements and not to cause any type of hindrance; close-fitting sweaters, elasticized trousers, vests or jackets that do not cover the holster and magazine pouches, and so on. We are well aware that, instead, normal clothing that we wear every day is not like that. In order to learn the rudiments of real-life defense operational shooting, we must thus accustom ourselves to apply every technique, and first of all the draw, taking our standard clothing and its relative limitations into account.

We should bear in mind that most civilian pistol carry permits are concealed-carry permits (although there are a number of states in the United States that allow weapons to be carried openly); in other words, it is obligatory to conceal (cover) the weapon and holster under your clothing. The reason for this rule is to avoid causing any alarm on the part of others. The price that has to be paid is an added degree of complication compared to those, such as the police, who are authorized to carry a weapon openly.

With regard to the draw itself, it can be somewhat hindered by an item of clothing such as a jacket, a sweater, or even a T-shirt if worn outside the trousers. How is the gun drawn when wearing such an item of clothing? The solution is not really complicated, you just have to understand it and perform it at will. In this respect we can distinguish roughly two categories of wearing apparel; those that are open in front or with flaps that can be opened (jackets, overcoats, topcoats, etc.) and those that are closed and that have to be lifted (sweaters, pullovers, shirts, etc.). The latter category obviously poses problems if worn outside the trousers.

- Jacket, coat, or any type of outer garment that is open in the front: the technique is very similar to the standard we have just described, with only a small modification, or better, accentuation of the initial movement of the strong hand. At the beginning of the movement (see preceding section, point 2) the right hand travels horizontally from the center of the chest to the side, so as to move aside the garment's flap with the back of the thumb (*Figure 4.18*); it then drops down along the side until it grasps the pistol grip (*Figure 4.19*). During all of this movement the jacket flap is kept far from the hand and arm, which are always in contact with the body.

- Sweater, T-shirt, shirt, or any type of closed garment (without a flap opening) worn outside the trousers: in this case, the technique is slightly different. At the beginning of the movement, the left hand travels diagonally to grasp the edge of the garment that is covering the holster, grasps the edge, and lifts it

Figures 4.18 and 4.19: Drawing from under an open jacket.

Figures 4.20 and 4.21: Drawing from under a shirt or sweater.

smartly towards the center of the chest (*Figure 4.20*). The right hand then grasps the weapon, draws it, and brings it up and forward, as shown in the standard technique. The left hand lets go of the garment, grasps the slide, and holds it firmly while the right hand pushes the pistol forward to rack it (*Figure 4.21*). From this point on, the standard technique is followed.

It is clear that the discussion does not end here. We can provide a few specific suggestions, by way of example. For example, during the winter months, if we are wearing a long jacket (a "three-quarter length" which covers down to the thighs), we often keep the front buttoned up. The coat may be closed by using buttons, snap closures, or a zipper, but in any case, it would be slow to open to make the first type of draw (to open the flap) but, at the same time, the weight and stiffness of the jacket are such as to make the second type of draw (lifting an edge) difficult if not impossible. What to do, then?

Well then, it is advisable to avoid a close-fitting and completely closed garment, and to opt for a variant that is comfortable and that is closed by buttons or whose zipper is the type that can be opened from either the top or the bottom (*Figure 4.22*). In this case, by keeping the bottom of the jacket partly open, it is possible to perform the standard draw, pushing back the jacket flap with the right hand while we are reaching to grasp the pistol, just as though it were a jacket that is only slightly heavier than a normal suit jacket (*Figure 4.23*).

That was just a simple example to underscore the fact that we should not get stuck on procedures in a passive and mechanical way, but should force ourselves to find solutions to every possible hitch and variation. Far from claiming to exhaust all possibilities, this book is aimed at stimulating the reader's intuitiveness and inquisitiveness (which cannot be separated, as we often repeat, from constant practice at the range under the direction of expert and qualified instructors).

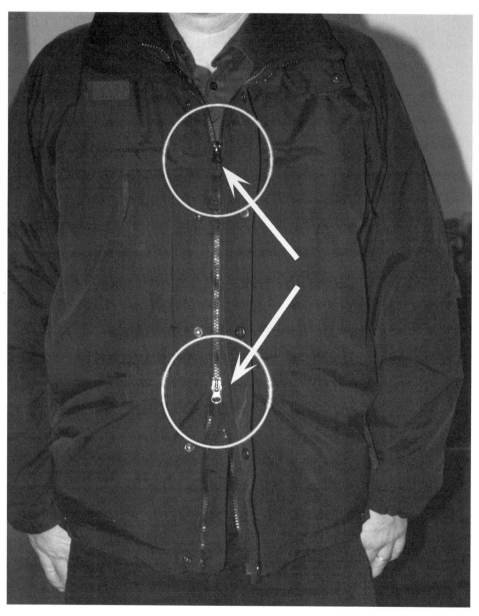

Figure 4.22: A double slider zipper, open at both top and bottom.

Figure 4.23: Drawing while moving aside the lower flap.

CHAPTER 5
FIRING POSITIONS

In this chapter we will examine various firing positions: standing, kneeling, seated, prone, etc. We will be dealing with basic information, rather than an exhaustive study. The important thing is to assimilate some basic principles, so as to be able to carry them over into real-life situations with all of the relative "ingredients" of uncertainty and surprise.

Firing Position versus Combat Position

For the sake of simplicity we will talk about firing positions, but as we have already said and as we shall later underline again in the book, from an operational viewpoint of real-life defense, it is more exact to speak of combat positions.

The Israeli operational approach is based on the consideration that in a real-life defense shooting scenario, we cannot precisely separate the firing from other defensive dimensions and actions, including a hand-to-hand encounter. Such a precise distinction would be completely artificial, because reality is itself unpredictable and chaotic. In reality it can happen that we are opening fire on an attacker and suddenly we are attacked by an accomplice who throws himself upon us bodily, or we are surrounded by people who are fleeing in panic and who bump into us or who grab hold of us, and so on. Defense is combat, and not just "shooting."

It is for this reason that the Israeli school teaches positions which, on the one hand, are very simple and optimize our instinctive reactions to danger and, on the other hand, are solid, full of tension, and "multi-purpose"—that is, they are useful both for shooting as well as to react against unexpected developments, to be able to move quickly, protect ourselves, or to counterattack in an unexpected fistfight, etc.

Firing While Standing

The basic firing position is this (*Figure 5.1*); facing the target, legs spread and flexed (under tension), feet parallel, arms extended towards the target, two-handed grip on the weapon (thumbs folded and on top of each other), head slightly pulled down to the shoulders, both eyes open and focused on the target. It is a position that in some classic shooting schools is called the "isosceles position." The Israeli school does not attribute that name to it, because it is not assumed consciously, formally, precisely, or for stylistic reasons, but instead is a reference position (with due tolerance for necessary variations) in which we find ourselves following instinctive psychophysical reactions, and we thus take advantage of it to assume an immediate defensive reaction.

Figure 5.1: Standing firing position.

There are two aspects to be underscored here (aside from the method of grasping the weapon, which we have analyzed in the previous chapter); the front-facing position and flexing the legs.

Frontal position: facing the target, with both eyes open, allows us to have the widest view of the scene possible. To the contrary, assymetrical positions, to the side or three-quarters, such as the classic Weaver position (*Figure 5.2*) considerably lessen both the perception of the surroundings as well as 360-degree reaction ability, and thus based on our experience we have found the above described position to be more functional. There are also American research statistics that show how even operators trained to adopt the Weaver position, in the event of an unexpected firefight, instinctively assume a front-facing position (isosceles, specifically) at a rate of about ninety percent.

Flexing the legs: legs flexed under tension respond, on one hand, to our body's instinctive defensive reaction, which tenses in the face of unexpected danger and, on the other hand, to the need to be ready to react and to be ready to spring, to rotate, move, duck, etc. If the legs are extended normally (straight) and relaxed, our position is fine for target shooting with concentration and precision. But if we are under stress and have to shoot to defend ourselves and be ready to face a threat from 360 degrees, our legs have to be charged and full of intense potential energy. It is not by chance, in any sport,

Figure 5.2: Assymetrical, side and three-quarter positions like the so-called Weaver position do not allow for 360-degree perception and reaction.

when an athlete has to be ready to spring with an explosive reaction that he assumes a position similar to this. We will come back to address this very important point in greater depth in the final chapter of this book.

Naturally, we are presenting here a general rule which, as with any rule, can have exceptions; it is obvious that in some circumstances and surroundings the position will have to be modified and adapted according to the situation. Let's imagine ourselves to be inside a bus or a subway car, or in a crowded hallway, or on rocky ground that is unstable, etc.; we certainly cannot assume a perfectly head-on position identical to the one that is pictured. But that does not change the fact that the basic principles are those that we have explained. To correctly learn the basic position allows us, as needed, to adapt it effectively and functionally, for example by placing one leg in front of the other to better take advantage of the space available.

Firing While Kneeling

At times it can be appropriate to crouch down and fire while kneeling; this can be done to take advantage of a low item of shelter (like a small wall), to reduce our silhouette and make ourselves less vulnerable, and/or to be more stable and take better aim when the threat is at medium to long-range.

Figure 5.3: Kneeling firing position.

The kneeling position taught by the Israeli school is as follows: the body is facing forward with the arms pointing towards the target; the knee of the strong leg (that is, that of the side of the hand that is holding the weapon) rests on the ground; the foot is bent with the toes resting on the ground; the gluteus rests on the heel; the other leg is thrust forward, with the bottom of the foot resting firmly on the ground (*Figure 5.3*). To assume the kneeling position, starting from a standing position, the weak (left) leg is brought forward and you drop onto the strong (right) knee.

We would underscore the following aspects: the stability of this position, and that the movement while getting into the crouch always leans forward:

Stability: When we get down on our knee, we are firing while seated on the heel of our strong (right) leg whenever possible (*Figure 5.3b*). This position is steady and very stable. Even if we were to be bumped from the side or rear, we would likely not lose our balance, or we would regain it very quickly.

To the contrary, if we were to have our gluteus lifted away from our heel, if we were semi-raised and leaning forward, a push or shove would cause us to lose our balance radically, causing us to fall or forcing us to put our hands on the ground for balance, thus seriously compromising our defensive reaction. Operational experience has led us to choose, from among the various possible kneeling positions, the one which we have described above as it offers the best possible mix of stability, comfort, and effectiveness. We can easily test all of this: without a weapon, try to get down on your knee in the way we have described and ask a friend or colleague to push you from one side or from the rear; we will see how relatively easy it is to keep our balance and to regain it instantly. Let's then try to kneel in a different position, for example, keeping ourselves raised rather than resting on our heel, and repeat the test; inevitably we will put one or both of our hands on the ground in order to avoid falling to the ground. We can also try to maintain these different positions for a long period of time, and we will easily find out the different comfort level and ability to maintain our position between the two. Still with respect to stability, the forward leg should be kept bent at roughly ninety degrees, that is, with the tibia and the calf as perpendicular as possible to the ground. If we were to hold our leg too far forward, not only would we tend to be less stable but, in the confusion and heat of a real engagement, something or someone running past us could strike our leg violently, causing pain, potential physical harm, distraction, and loss of balance.

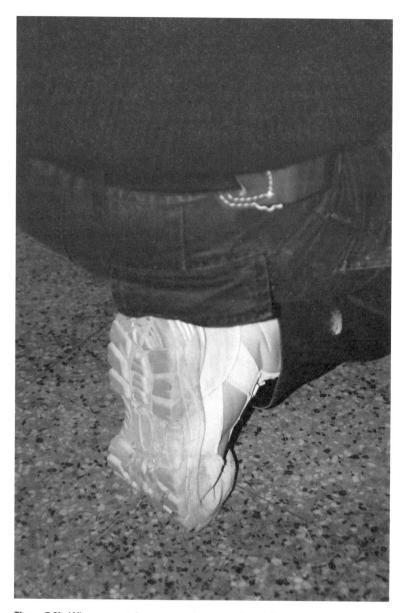

Figure 5.3b: When we get down on our knee, we fire while seated on the heel of the strong (right) leg when possible; this way our position is gathered and very stable. Even if we were to be pushed, we would be able to easily keep our balance, or at worse be able to regain it quickly. On the other hand, if we were to keep ourselves raised off of our heel, it would be very easy to fall and/or rest our hands on the ground after being pushed.

Leaning forward to kneel: We have already said that to assume the kneeling position the left leg is put forward, rather than pulling the right leg to the rear. Why? Because in reality the space around us is not clear, ordered, and antiseptic as it is on a firing range. In a real-life situation there can be a thousand possible obstacles around and behind us. We can see what is in front of us, but not what is in back of us. To shift a leg to the rear could cause us to bump into something, to slip, to snag on something, to lose our balance, with potentially ruinous consequences, not only and not so much because of the risk of falling but also because we would be caught off balance and defenseless against the threat. For this reason the Israeli operational approach teaches to make every movement, move, or pivot always to the front and never to the rear (except, obviously, in situations where forward movement is not practical).

Firing While Seated

If a threat should appear unexpectedly while we are seated, often there is no time to get up and assume one of the combat positions described above. Therefore we have to be capable to react and fire from the seated position:

1. Imagine that you are seated in a relaxed position, for example in a restaurant chair, theater seat, a seat on a bus, a bench in the park, etc. (*Figure 5.4*).

2. As soon as we identify the threat, we bend our legs at about ninety degrees, spread wide and firmly planted on the ground, as tense as though they were two springs and, at the same time, we lean our body forward (pelvis and bust) towards the forward edge of the seat. Our arms help us to make this rapid movement, using our elbows to push against the armrests (if present) or against the back of the seat, and then assume the position that precedes the draw itself; the left hand travels up to the chest, while the right hand travels down vertically towards the pistol grip (*Figure 5.5*).

3. We draw the pistol and bring it towards our right hand, which has risen to the level of the sternum or the throat (*Figure 5.6*) and then rack the weapon at eye level, energetically pointing the weapon towards the threat, as we have seen in detail in the chapter dealing with draw techniques (*Figure 5.7*).

4. With both arms extended towards the threat and both hands grasping the pistol (the left hand wraps around the right and the thumbs are squeezed together, as explained in the chapter dealing with the draw) we are ready to shoot (*Figure 5.8*).

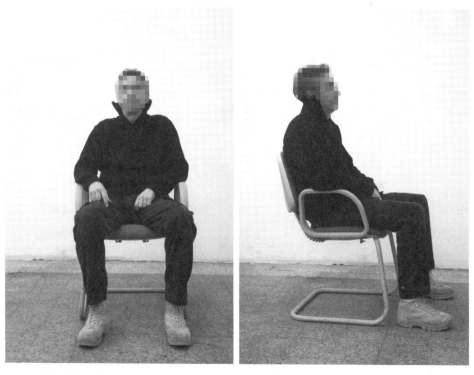

Figure 5.4: Initial position: relaxed and stretched out on a chair.

After having fired the first few rounds from this position, if necessary (and if possible), we should stand up with the utmost speed and continue the combat engagement while standing. Once we are on our feet we will have a better view of the scene and will be able to identify the presence of any other threats.

Naturally, even this technique is a basic standard, which must be adapted to the thousands of unforeseen variables in a real engagement. If, for example, we are sitting in our car, it is clear that drawing the weapon will be hindered by cramped spaces and normal impediments (steering wheel, safety belt, the door) and depending on where we are seated; when seated in a car, it is advisable to move and slightly modify

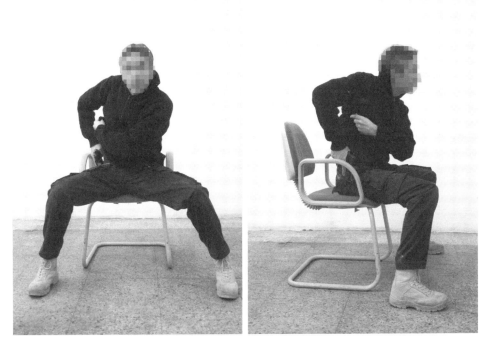

Figure 5.5: Immediate reaction to the threat: we lean towards the edge of the chair, legs tensed, arms and hands ready to draw the weapon.

Figures 5.6 and 5.7: Drawing and racking while remaining seated.

Figure 5.8: Pointing the weapon, ready to fire.

the position of the holster in order to make any draw easier, insofar as possible; in case of need, to accomplish the draw you have to lean forward a bit away from the back of the seat.

The speed of movement will never be equal to that of a "normal," less complex situation (for example, while seated at a table in a restaurant), but we have to be realistic and dismiss the myth of extreme speed as an end in itself.

We'll repeat it yet again: there is no technique or speed of execution which, in and of itself, can give us a mathematical certainty that we will be safe from all danger; reality is complicated, fleeting, unforeseeable, and the only real solution is on the one hand to learn the techniques to the best degree possible but, on the other hand, to be always alert and ready to face surprises with intelligence, decisiveness, determination, and flexibility.

Firing While Prone

Also with regard to other anomalous combat positions, such as firing from the prone position, we want again to repeat the usual basic premise: we should not concentrate on seeking the "pure" technique, or the "perfect" position. We apologize if we seem pedantic, but the repetition of this concept is intentional. We want to stress and re-stress this point: the important thing is to acquire the proper combat mentality—technique is an important complement to be sure, but is not enough in itself and, in some senses, is not even the primary element.

We are in an operational defense shooting environment, and in this context what counts to save our life and possibly that of someone near us is our reaction time, proper identification of the threat or threats, and the speed and intensity of our response; these are the essential elements for an effective defense. Technique counts, to be sure, but you have to learn certain basic fundamentals, and in the crucial moment it is not necessary (nor, almost ever, possible) to apply it one hundred percent. It could be enough to be able to apply only seventy percent of the technique, but a one hundred percent reaction is necessary. The brain reacts, and the body and the technique follow it.

Thus, before describing firing from the prone position we have to ask ourselves why, how, and under what circumstances we might find ourselves lying down; firing from a lying position is not "nice," it is not an exercise of skill or athletic ability, it is only a very disadvantageous position in which we might find ourselves involuntarily forced by circumstances. In the context of real-life defense, a thousand unpredictable things can make us fall: an argument, running or a clumsy movement, a stumble, bumping up against a person, object, or vehicle, etc. We could thus find ourselves lying on the ground and, faced with an immediate danger, we might not have the time to get up, and we would be forced to react immediately while on the ground, right where we are.

Already in these first few fractions of a second, from the instant we find ourselves on the ground, we understand the crucial importance of having our mind ready and reactive: it will not be only the technique that saves our skin but most of all the immediacy with which our brain is able to evaluate the situation. If we were to make the wrong choice, like trying to get up, flee, and take cover in the face of an armed opponent ready to fire, there would be no technique that could protect us. If the threat is really looming over us, it is useless and counterproductive to try to get ourselves out of the situation (when on the ground our movements are obviously slower) and the right choice is to react with fire with the utmost speed. Only later, after having hit or at least placed the attacker under pressure, can we find a moment to get up and assume a more advantageous position. If this context is understood, we hope that the reason is clear why we say that intelligence and reactive ability count for much more than does the technique in and of itself.

Having said that, let us look at some practical aspects relating to shooting while lying flat in various positions (remember that we are not dealing with a position that we have voluntarily chosen, but are coping with an accidental condition imposed on us):

Lying on your back (*Figure 5.9*): To be lying on your back is probably the least disadvantageous of all of these situations, because it allows some degree of visual awareness and of reactivity (for example, if we were lying on a bed we would be

Figure 5.9: Firing while lying on your back.

Figure 5.10: Firing while lying on the weak side.

able to get up much more quickly than we would if we were lying on our stomach). To shoot while lying on our back we assume a taut, tensed combat position (just as when we are on our feet, although the proportions will vary): our legs are bent, the flats of our feet are on the ground if possible, head and shoulders partly raised almost as though we were exercising our abdominal muscles, arms extended forward and pointing the pistol. Keeping our legs bent and thus partly raised affords us stability and the ability to react, and hinders our view only to a certain extent. You can try lying on your back and looking at your surroundings through the "V" formed by your legs (a sort of rear sight notch in a large format); you will easily see that you have an almost complete view of the area in front of you (both horizontally as well as vertically). We do not keep our legs extended because we are not engaging in a sporting exercise nor are we relaxed; our legs need to be tensed like springs, ready for any eventuality.

Lying on your weak side (*Figure 5.10*): If we are lying on our weak side (let us assume that it is the left side) our legs also in this case assume a tense and reactive position. The weak (left) leg rests on the ground but is pointed forward and bent so that the foot is close to the pelvis.

The strong (right) leg is raised and bent, with the flat of the foot resting on the ground. The legs thus form a sort of triangle, and from this position we are ready to roll on the ground and get up relatively quickly (getting on our knee) with the aid of the weak arm. While we are lying in this position, the weak (left) arm is resting on the ground from the shoulder to the elbow, and bends slightly while raising the forearm off the ground in order to support and adequately grasp the strong hand that is grasping the weapon. The strong (right) arm is taut and pointed at the target, as in the standard firing position.

Lying on your strong side (*Figure 5.11*): If we are lying on our strong (let us assume it is the right) side, the legs assume the same position as just described, obviously as a mirror image of when we are lying on our opposite side: the strong (right) leg in contact with the ground and bent, and the weak (left) leg raised and bent with the foot resting on the ground. The shoulder of the strong arm is resting on the ground but is pointed towards the threat, the weak arm flexes as much as needed to provide support for a two-handed grip. In case of extreme need, naturally, you can fire from the ground using only one hand.

Figure 5.11: Firing while lying on the strong side.

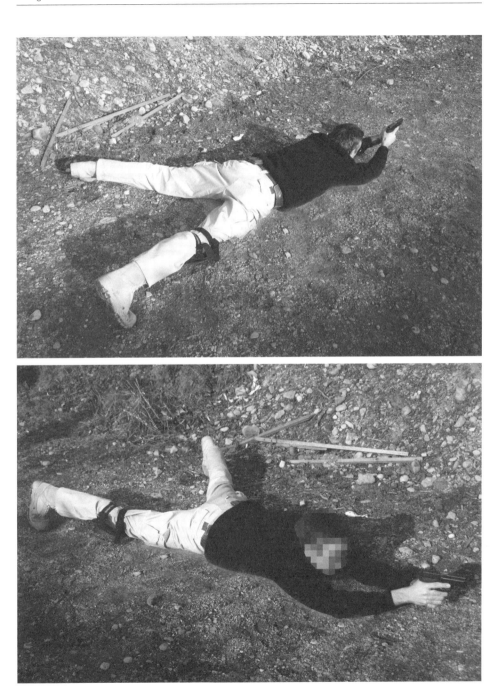

Figure 5.12: Firing while lying on the stomach.

Lying on your stomach (*Figure 5.12*): Finding ourselves lying on our stomach is not comfortable, nor is it advantageous (remember that we are speaking of a situation of defense with a handgun, and not of target shooting or sniping at long range with a rifle). It is not comfortable because it is very tiring to tense (and to keep tense for some time) our back muscles, to raise our head and shoulders higher than our abdomen. It is also disadvantageous because is significantly reduces our field of view and radius of action; compared to when we are lying on our back, the ability to move our head and thus to see is limited both horizontally and most of all, vertically. Thus, as we have said already, this position is not a choice, but if we find ourselves in such a condition we nevertheless must react. Try to keep your legs spread for greater stability.

We keep our feet firmly pointed to the ground, not relaxed (*Figure 5.13*) because this must also, as always, be a reactive combat position. Point the arms forward while holding the weapon towards the threat. Depending on the circumstances, we might need to raise ourselves up a bit on our elbows, and thus partially bend our arms, to aim and fire in the necessary direction. Alternatively, we could rest our weak hand on the ground and fire using only our strong hand. As soon as possible, that is as soon as there is a pause or slowdown by the attacker (having hit him or otherwise put him under pressure), we should take the opportunity to assume a safer and more manageable position.

When you fire from a prone position, everything becomes more complicated, even changing a magazine when you run out of rounds. In the chapter dedicated to changing magazines we will see how to act under such circumstances to avoid or cope with any difficulties.

Unconventional Positions (Firing from the Side)

Normally the shooting technique calls for extending our arms in front of us, pointing the weapon towards the target. In some cases, however, we have to adopt a less visible, unconventional firing position. Let's imagine a situation in which the attacker is momentarily distracted (he is pointing his weapon at us but is looking elsewhere) or is in a position with respect to which we are partly under cover or in defilade (he is threatening us and other people near us with his weapon; spouse , colleague, salesperson, etc.). In this case we might have the opportunity to draw our own weapon and fire, if conditions require and allow it, but we should avoid calling the attacker's attention to our movements.

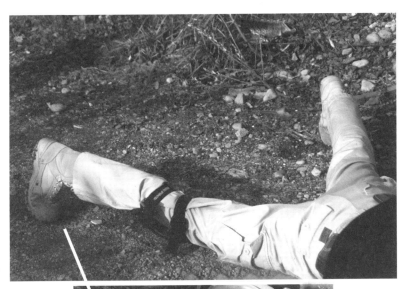

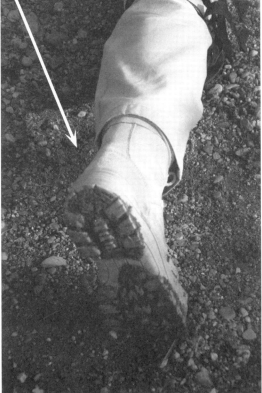

Figure 5.13: Note the feet firmly dug into the ground, even when we are lying in this position.

We therefore have to draw our pistol without changing our position and limiting our movements to the minimum indispensable (Note: This type of technique implies that the threat is at a relatively close distance, as aiming must be completely instinctive and thus cannot be particularly accurate):

- The right hand grasps the weapon, drawing it only as much as is needed to aim it towards the threat, but without lifting it to chest level; the pistol thus remains level with our side, with the muzzle pointing towards the target;

- The left hand travels along the bust but also stays low, roughly at the level of the abdomen, until it reaches the weapon along our right side, and there the slide is racked to chamber a round; the racking is done with a quick movement, less visible than the standard mode;

- Shooting is directly from the side (or hip), without raising the weapon (*Figure 5.14*); if our movements have been quick and discreet enough, the attacker or attackers will have some difficulty in reacting before it is too late.

It should be noted, among other things, that this is one of the reasons why operational shooting pistols fitted with compensators are not advisable; firing from the hip, the muzzle flash and reside generated from the shot and that escapes upward from the compensator slots might distract us or, in the worst case, even wound us.

One-Handed Firing

We have seen that the standard firing technique calls for a two-handed grasp of the weapon. There are, however, situations in which that is not possible (as we have already mentioned in an earlier chapter). We discussed one of the more typical cases in the preceding section; shooting from the side or hip must of necessity be done with one hand only. But there are other cases when we have neither the time nor the ability to grasp the pistol with both hands, and thus it is inevitable that we have to fire it using only one hand.

Figure 5.14: Firing from the hip (the finger is intentionally on the trigger to show that this is not a rest position but rather a firing position).

For example, the attacker might surprise us at close range. He could be not directly in front of us but on our strong side (the side that carries our weapon). He might not be stationary but could approach us very quickly. In these cases we have barely enough time to draw and chamber a round and have to open fire quickly, without being able to adopt the classic two-handed grip; to fire immediately gives us a fraction of a second's advantage, which could make all the difference. In addition, having one hand free could prove to be advantageous under certain conditions. When we fire with only one hand, we must be aware of the following conditions:

- The hand that is grasping the weapon must hold it very tightly, with the thumb bent and firmly closed around the pistol grip. As we have seen in the chapter dealing with the proper grasp and the draw, closing the thumbs around the weapon is important to maintain a firm grip even in cases of a close-in attack and attempts to seize your weapon; if a firm grasp is important when we are

Figure 5.15: One-handed firing.

holding our weapon with both hands, it is obviously even more important when we are using only one hand.

- The other hand is normally extended diagonally forward and facing outward (*Figure 5.15*), for three reasons: balance, protection, and reaction. Balance: the arm extended to our front helps us to maintain balance. Protection: arm and hand can act to protect other persons near us or to protect ourselves (from pushes or shoves, of from other assailants who attack us with their bare hands or with a club or knife, etc.). Reaction: by having our hand extended in front of us, almost parallel to the hand holding the pistol, we need only an instant to join our hands and assume the two-handed stance (which is undoubtedly more stable) when we get the chance.

In the final chapter of the book we will address some additional considerations concerning the one-handed stance, seeking to address any doubts and provide answers.

CHAPTER 6

MULTIPLE TARGETS AND VARYING DISTANCES

The true battlefield is three-dimensional, it is not flat like a TV screen or the bench at a target range. The distance to the targets (which in reality are armed and dangerous targets) has a basic tactical relevance. What we have to take into account in a real-life defense scenario is the distance of the targets from us as well as the distance between them, as well as the effective danger that each poses (as a function of distance and other factors). All of this influences our shooting technique, our movements, and our rate of fire.

Multiple Targets: Engagement Priority

Above all, when we face multiple attackers, we have to react based on a scale of priorities. Which target should we engage first? If we were to react at random, without making a proper selection by priority, we would seriously risk engaging the "wrong" target first and be overwhelmed by other attackers. Our instinct could lead us to shoot first at the threat closest to us, but it is not a given that this would be the right choice. The criteria to establish target priority is not simply their distance from us, but their effective danger, of which distance is undoubtedly a factor but not the only one. To simplify, we might say that the danger posed by an attacker is a combination of two factors: distance and offensive potential (which in turn depends on the weapon, capability, mobility, etc.). Let's look at a few examples. Let's imagine that we are coping with two attackers, located at different distances from us, and with different offensive potentials:

- An attacker six to seven yards away, armed with a knife, and an attacker twenty yards away armed with a rifle; based on our experience the more dangerous threat, and thus the threat to be dealt with first, is the second attacker who, even though further away, is armed with a rifle and could hit us before the other attacker could reach us with his knife; in this case then the offensive potential is relatively independent of the distance;

- An attacker two to three yards away armed with a knife, and an attacker fifteen yards away armed with a pistol; at such a short distance, less than four yards, an attacker armed with a knife is extremely dangerous and can reach us and stab us seriously in only a few seconds (a time potentially less than that of the other attacker to take aim and fire on us from around fifteen yards away, which is not a trivial distance for a shooter who is not well trained); therefore in this case we should immediately engage the first attacker, as in this case the theoretically less dangerous weapon (the knife) is in reality the source of a priority offensive power due to the short distance from us;

- An attacker six to seven yards away armed with a knife, and an attacker six to seven yards away armed with a pistol, which is jammed; the most imminent threat might appear to be from the knife, especially if the attacker is rushing towards us quickly, but to clear a jam takes only a few moments if the person knows how to clear it, so let's not be distracted by the attacker with the knife. The other threat, even though the attacker may not make any obvious moves, could, in this case, be much more lethal; the conclusion is; always keep an open mind and always reason logically, as quickly as possible, and do not let your assessment be conditioned by microscopic considerations (at times what is least obvious may be the most lethal).

We could continue this discussion with other similar examples, but the important thing to note, aside from all of the outlines and simplifications for the sake of a clear example, is to understand the basic rule: we must always use our primary weapon, that is, our brain; we have to develop our capability to acquire and identify the target or targets and thus engage the more dangerous target first, which is not necessarily the closest target. Based on the specific situation we will be able to understand which is the most dangerous threat, and therefore the priority (*Figures 6.1 a, b, c*).

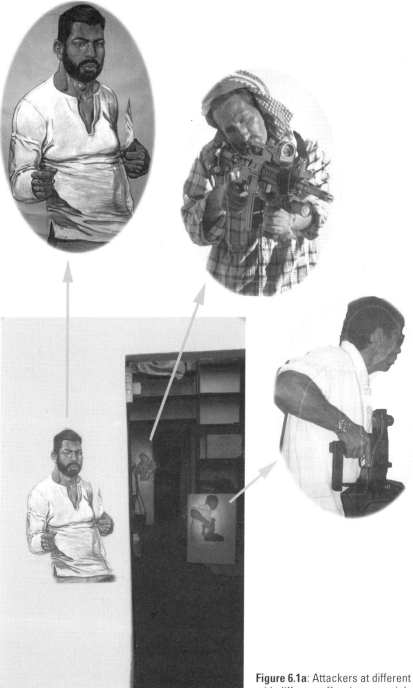

Figure 6.1a: Attackers at different distances with different offensive potential.

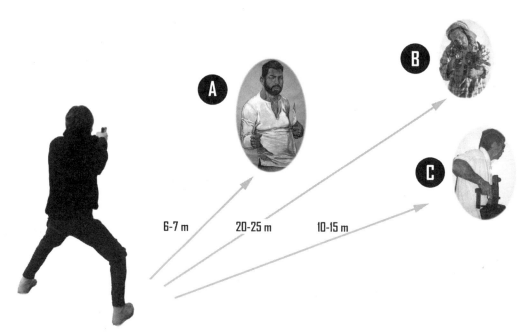

Figure 6.1b: Let us imagine the following scenario: At a distance of about six to seven meters we have aggressor A, armed with a knife. At a distance of about twenty to twenty-five meters is aggressor B armed with a rifle pointed towards us. At a distance of about ten to fifteen meters is aggressor C with another firearm which he is in the process of drawing and/or which is not pointed at us. Which threat should be considered the priority? According to our approach, the priority depends not only on distance but on a combination of two factors: distance and offensive potential. In this case then we would immediately engage aggressor B with several shots in quick succession, then aggressor A with one or two rounds, and then C. If necessary, we would then fire additional shots at the threat or threats that are still active. It is only an example, which is of necessity simplified, and as always should not be taken as gospel; our brain has to work quickly and evaluate each case on its own merits. We wish again to repeat the irreplaceable importance of continuing training that is realistic and is taught by qualified and expert instructors who can guarantee both the effectiveness and safety of the training exercises.

It is superfluous to add that each target can be engaged repeatedly: once the first target has been engaged, we turn to the second, then back to the first if necessary, and so on. It could be dangerous and counterproductive to focus on one target after another based on a purely "mechanical" sequence; a real-life engagement is not like a target range or a videogame where we can knock down the targets one after another in an orderly fashion, like knocking down tenpins. In reality an attacker who is hit might not fall, or can get back up, or in any case might still pose an active threat. On the

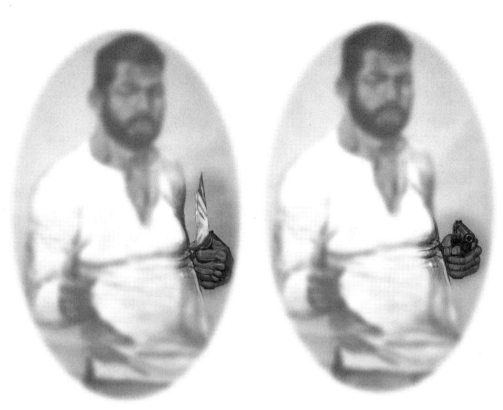

Figure 6.1c: Evaluation of priorities when engaging a threat always has to take into account the distance as well as the offensive potential. At equal distances, obviously, much changes if the assailant has a knife or if he has a pistol. In this figure we see two different offensive potentials, simulating the tunnel vision effect under combat stress.

other hand, if we remained focused on a single target, hitting it until it was completely neutralized, the other attacker or attackers could in the meantime attack us and have the better of us. Let us therefore engage the priority target with one or more shots, based on need, in order to neutralize him (if we are able to) or at least put him under pressure, injure him, and remove him from continuing his attack; then we shift to the second target and after having also hit it, we shift back to the first target to determine if he has to be hit again, until we have totally eliminated the threat. Here we would like to underscore a few points. First, we must know the rules and techniques and hold them dear, but without locking us into fixed schemes; the examples we have given (distance, weapons, etc.) have only an approximate value. In reality, only one small detail can completely change the scenario and the priorities. The advice is the same as always: keep your attention sharp and work your brain to the utmost. The right decision cannot be determined in an abstract and absolute manner; we can only make it there, in the field, in that crucial moment, rapidly evaluating all of the factors that are in play. Second, we must not only keep ourselves alert but must also keep our eyes wide open, and not just in a manner of speaking. In fact, it is precisely in this type of situation that the essential importance of keeping both eyes open can be best appreciated; to close one eye for more than a moment to take careful aim at one of the attackers might mean losing sight of the other or others. In the excitement of the moment, to cut our field of view in half could be a fatal error.

How to Engage Targets That Are Close to Each Other

When two targets are close to each other (imagine two attackers side by side or only a short distance away from each other), to shift from one target to the other we only

Figure 6.2: A "V" movement to engage two targets close to each other.

have to move our pistol along the horizontal plane, from left to right or vice-versa. Nevertheless, if this move were linear, our line of sight would be in reality imprecise and "dancing"; it is very easy that, under stress, these apparently simple operations become forced, shaky, and not very accurate. It is even easy to miss the target completely if the distance is not very close; we only need to make an exaggerated or involuntary movement because of the tension we are under and we miss the second target, and just an instant later, have to realign our weapon on him. It's enough of a pause to lose precious time and, in the worst case, to end up in serious trouble. Based on field experience, the Israeli school has found a simple expedient that can significantly increase the accuracy of a multiple engagement. Rather than to move the weapon horizontally, we make a small "V" movement (*Figure 6.2*):

- The weapon is aimed at the first target; to shift to the second target, you do not move laterally but rather diagonally downwards.

- Then the weapon is raised to the center of the second target, tracing a "V" or a "U" in the air.

This movement, naturally, is very fast and is quite restricted in its arc; it is just enough to break up the linearity of the movement and does not suffer the "sliding" effect typical of a condition of high psychophysical stress.

How to Engage Targets That Are Far from Each Other

When two targets are at a medium-far distance from each other, the "V" movement we have just described is not enough and we have to make a very pronounced move to shift from one to the other. Even in this case, if we were to keep the weapon pointed in front of us, moving it horizontally from the first to the second target, while at the same time having to change our own position, the dislocation would be such that it would seriously compromise the accuracy of fire. What follows is the technique adopted by the Israeli school (*Figure 6.3*):

- Engage the first target, then pull the pistol slightly towards our chest (similar to when we get ready to rack the weapon while drawing) while we shift our gaze to look at the second attacker;

Figure 6.3: To engage targets that are far from each other, we take rapid steps forward and to the side, pulling our weapon close to our chest and then pointing it at the second target.

- With the outer leg (that is, the leg opposite the second target: the right leg if the target is to the left, and vice-versa) we make a quick step forward and to the side in order to assume as much of a frontal position as possible with respect to the new target, all the while maintaining our combat positions (legs spread and tensed, low center of gravity);

- While we execute this movement, we thrust our arms forward again, pointing the weapon at the new target, ready to fire; aiming is instinctive and effective with this method, and is not affected by being thrown off target as we have mentioned.

It should be noted that our movements are always forward, never to the rear. As we have already said, we know what is in front of us, but not what is behind us; by moving forward we avoid making a bad move by stumbling or bumping into an obstacle that could cause us to lose our balance or even make us fall, which during a firefight could have obviously serious consequences.

Distance and Rate of Fire

We have to adjust our rate of fire based on the distance to the target. When a target is quite far from us (for example, twenty yards or more, always assuming that we are speaking of firing with a handgun) we adopt a slower rate of fire to improve accuracy; at such a distance we can engage in aimed fire rather than just pointed fire, that is, we can briefly close one eye, and slow fire helps us to better control our weapon and make our shots more effective; in addition, the distance itself complicates the attacker's offensive action and relieves the pressure on us. In other words, the distance makes a slower rate of fire than normal possible as well as advisable. As the distance drops, the rate of fire increases; the closer the target, the more rapid our fire should be.

Imagining three targets at increasing distance from us, let's say five yards, ten yards and twenty yards, when we engage the first target our rate of fire should be very rapid (a sort of "ba-bam!"), engaging the second target it will slow down a bit ("bam! bam!"), and engaging the third target it will be even slower and more accurate ("bam… bam…").

CHAPTER 7

MOVING AND USE OF COVER

Defense and combat are dynamic, confused, and frenetic dimensions. It is indispensable to know how to move properly, to alternate between brisk moves and quick stops, to use any cover available, etc.; this chapter is dedicated to these subjects (some details will be covered more in depth in chapter 10).

Mental Attitude and Movement

In the preceding chapters we have had reason to stress more than once that, in the Israeli approach to operational and defense shooting, we do not speak of the "firing position" but of the "combat position." Even when we consider so-called static situations, in which we fire while standing still, being static is never, in our view, a synonym for passivity or a relaxed stance; the position we assume for firing is only apparently "static" and is in reality, as we have already explained, a position charged with dynamism, of potential energy, ready for any type of supercharged explosive reaction (hand-to-hand combat, shifting positions, running, etc.).

Now we will extend this principle even further: we will speak not only of the "combat position" but, more in general, of "combat behavior." Our every action, our every move must be pervaded by this energy, always projected forward, towards and against the threat. We must remember the principle of the Israeli philosophy of security and defense: faced with an aggressor we should never feel as the prey, but must always transform ourselves into the predator. The positions we adopt for combat, the movements that we make on the ground where the encounter takes place, are all and always animated by this principle, by this controlled and channeled aggressiveness, by this desire to not give up but rather to win.

Even before any encounter (an event that we hope never happens to us), during training with or without weapons, and indeed during our daily lives, we should train ourselves and become accustomed to assume this "combat behavior," this bodily behavior. The weapon comes later, it is only a tool; it is our body and our attitude that have to be charged with energy and combativeness.

Naturally, combat behavior and an attitude that changes us from prey to predator require an even deeper and fundamental characteristic: a "combat mentality," the warrior spirit, warriorhood (which Grossman speaks of in the previously cited *On Combat*). We have said it before and will say it again: the first and most essential weapon is our brain. Everything else is an extension of it.

All of these principles reveal their importance and worth in a particular way when we pass the static training phase and face the training cycle in a dynamic setting or, heaven forbid, the reality of an actual encounter.

Walking, Running, Halting

The techniques regarding moving from one position to another are very simple: when you have to walk, you walk; when you have to run, you run. It sounds like a joke, but the implications are real. On the one hand, movements are made naturally (no bizarre movements, athletic feats, or fancy dance steps are needed) and, on the other hand, they should be imbued with aggressiveness and energy (we are not on a sightseeing tour, we are fighting to defend ourselves):

- Our moves should be natural: the more natural the movement, the quicker and more effective it will be, and relatively resistant to the effects of stress. Other schools teach particular techniques to walk, such as the "heel-toe," that are tied to the principle of firing while moving (the "strange" gait acts to minimize an unsteady weapon); it is a solution that we generally do not favor, as we will soon explain, as it would apply to only specific situations (professional operators in a wartime context, clearing out buildings, etc.). Because generally speaking we do not fire while moving, for us movement must be as natural as possible.

- Our moves should be combative: we have to move in a decisive, rapid, aggressive, tense, and aware manner. When we walk in a tactical situation (defense, an engagement under way, clearing an area, be it a street, a bus stop, or your back yard) we are not taking a leisurely walk but rather are moving decisively and with quick steps, remaining well aware of our surroundings (visual and audible). When we run, we have to run as fast as possible, sprinting like runners at a track meet or like a lion chasing its prey or attacking another animal that has ventured into its territory.

Three important notes apply to displacement moves: the first two have to do with safety and how to handle the weapon during the moves, and the third deals with how to fire while moving:

- While we are walking or running, our index finger has to absolutely remain outside the trigger guard and thus away from the trigger itself (*Figure 7.1*); it

Figure 7.1: During displacement, especially when running, it is imperative to keep the finger away from the trigger.

Figure 7.2: While walking or running, the weapon is kept by your side, pointing forward, without making it stick out too much to the side or to the front.

is the basic rule of safety, which is always valid, and is naturally even more important when we are moving, and which adds to the risk of involuntary hand movements.

- During the walk or run, we keep the weapon on our right side, pointing forward, close to the body and with our arm bent at about ninety degrees (*Figure 7.2*). Ideally, the weapon should stick out only as little as possible, both to the front as well as to the side. By holding the weapon this way, we guarantee the best compromise between ergonomics (we can walk or run freely, in a natural manner, without losing our balance), quick reaction (we can aim and fire in an instant), ability to hold on to our weapon (anyone who might try to wrest our pistol from us would meet with some degree of difficulty, whereas if we were to grasp it differently it would be more exposed), and even discretion (at times it is not advisable, for a host of reasons, to "wave the weapon about" in a highly visible manner.

- We habitually stop in order to fire. We usually do not fire while on the move, except under unusual conditions, because experience from years in the field has shown that firing while moving reduces accuracy and creates various problems (for example, in an operational scenario where there is a crowd present , such as at a station, an airport, etc.) that are greater than the advantage to be gained in terms of reaction speed.

- While in order to walk or run we rely on our natural instinct, there is a particular technique that we use to come to a halt. In a real-life defense situation if it is necessary to come to a complete stop, most of the time such a halt will be sudden, sharp, and abrupt because of the surprise appearance of a threat, an unplanned need to change direction, or to have to fire at an attacker. Unfortunately an abrupt stop can cause us problems.

When we are running, but even when we are only walking at a quick and decisive pace, to make an abrupt stop is a delicate action, not only because of the possible difficulty in properly aiming the weapon at the target because of shaking and wavering, but also due to the distinct possibility of slipping and losing our balance.

If we think about our day-to-day experiences, we realize that when we try to make a sudden stop from running at full speed, it is easy for our feet to lose their purchase on the ground; it is an inherent risk when making a sudden change from movement to a state of rest (inertial force) and is aggravated by shoes with smooth soles and/or by unstable ground conditions, which could be downhill or slippery (gravel, rain, mud, ice, snow, etc.). This is a scientific fact: if a vehicle is traveling at only 30–35 mph, it will need several yards to brake and make a sudden stop, and the same applies to the human body. Let's consider the effect of a panic stop with an ABS system; certainly, the system acts to simplify the driver's task, who only has to push forcefully on the brake pedal. But the purpose of the ABS is to prevent the wheels from locking up instantaneously (which would cause the vehicle to slide) and the braking process assumes a syncopated sequence, and the wheels are alternately braked and released with a "skipping" sensation very similar to that which we use when moving our feet in accordance with the Israeli school.

Usually, however, how does our body stop itself as quickly as possible? The spontaneous method to come to a stop generally consists of a sort of small jump with our feet parallel to each other, not unlike when making a slide stop while skiing. This, in our opinion, is the best way to risk slipping and sliding, especially when the ground conditions are unfavorable as we have just described. In daily life a slip might cause a laugh, but (aside from the risk of bone breakage) it could have much more serious consequences during a shooting engagement.

Because of this the Israeli school has developed a specific technique for stopping in a very short space and period of time, minimizing the risk of slipping and losing our balance. When we are running and have to make a sudden stop, we do not make a jump with both of our feet together but rather make a very quick series of "steps in place" with both legs: as though they were two spring-loaded pistons, we forcefully stomp them, alternating the two feet, until we have come to a complete halt (*Figure 7.3*). It is a very simple and surprisingly effective method; we can test it ourselves and will soon realize the difference, especially on difficult terrain such as a wet surface, on gravel, or on a long downhill slope of compacted earth.

Figure 7.3: The typical quick stop with the legs that "stomp" vertically.

Pivoting in Place

At the range the targets are very cooperative—they are all in front of us, lined up one after another. But in a real-life situation it can easily happen that the threat does not present itself fully to the front but can come from one side or from behind us. We are thus forced to pivot on ourselves to defend ourselves.

Anatomically speaking, we have two alternatives in order to pivot. Let's imagine for example that we have to turn to the left to face a threat from that side. In theory, to do that we can choose from two movements: move our left leg to the rear, or place our right leg forward.

The Israeli school teaches us to adopt the second alternative; we always (except for unique cases in which there are insurmountable physical impediments) pivot on our outermost leg, that is, the one opposite to the side towards which we want to turn. The other leg is never moved backwards. We have already explained the reason in other parts of the book, and it is two-fold:

- We know what we have in front of us, but not what is behind us; therefore we can move forward with relative assurance in a quick, automatic, and safe fashion, while if we move backwards we run the risk of stumbling and losing our balance;

- From a psychological standpoint, we must always react actively to a threat, attack the aggressor, and transform ourselves from prey to the predator; therefore, it is advisable to become accustomed to moving instinctively towards and against the attacker rather than to give in to an impulse to flee or to become passive.

Another important note: in any case, before moving your legs and body, move your head so that you can identify the threat and assess the situation.
The technically correct movement sequence is as follows (*Figures 7.4, 7.5, and 7.6*):

1. If you perceive a sign of risk off to one side, for example to the left, turn your head immediately to look; at the same time, your strong hand should reach for the weapon, keeping it in its holster.

2. If we determine that the threat is real, we pivot while shifting forward, like a compass, with the right leg pivoting on the left; at the same time we draw our weapon from its holster.

3. While we complete the pivot and assume the combat position oriented to face the threat frontally, we point the pistol while racking it to chamber a round and are ready to fire. We shoot only after having completed the movement and having established a solid firing position, and not during the movement itself, otherwise our fire would suffer in its accuracy.

Figure 7.4: Perceiving a threat on the right side; the head immediately turns to that direction and the strong hand reaches for the weapon in the holster (without drawing it until the threat has been positively identified).

If the threat comes from behind rather than from the side, the technique is the same but the pivot is obviously more extensive (having to cover a 180-degree arc rather than a ninety-degree arc). To turn to the right or to the left, first with your gaze and then with your body, depends on our initial perception as to where the threat is coming from, but is relatively unimportant; the important thing is to always pivot forward with the outer leg rather than backwards with the inner leg.

Naturally, we underscore the fact that every rule has its exceptions and every technique should be tailored with critical intelligence and quickness based on the individual circumstances. These are only outlines of basic techniques, like the "fundamentals" of any sport, they are perfected through training, taught by qualified instructors, and then are applied with flexibility and reactivity in a real-life situation.

Figure 7.5: Threat identified: the opposite leg pivots forward, while the draw is accomplished.

Figure 7.6: Completing the pivot, the slide is racked chambering a round and pointing the weapon towards the threat; we are ready to fire.

Use of Shelter

In a real armed defense scenario in normal geographic conditions, it is rather improbable that an encounter would occur in a void, in a flat and uniform land (like a stretch of desert or a snowy field, or like a typical firing range). In a real situation, in town or in our own home, there are places that offer shelter which, in some cases, we can take advantage of to protect ourselves even partially while we respond to the fire of one or more attackers; doors, partitions, furniture, walls, vehicles, trees, building corners, barrels, crates, etc.

We must however make a general distinction between "shelter" and "cover"; this might seem to be a purely technical distinction, but it has an absolutely practical, in fact vital, applicability. A shelter is a shelter if it is bulletproof, that is, if it cannot be penetrated all the way through by an attacker's bullets and thus protects us in the strict sense of the word. Cover instead protects us from being seen, allows us to go into defilade or to hide, but does not protect us from bullets fired in our direction. Let's look at a few specific examples to better explain the difference:

Figure 7.7: A large diameter tree trunk can provide good shelter, while a hedge offers only cover.

Figure 7.8: A reinforced concrete wall is an excellent shelter, while a thin party wall of sheetrock or in some cases even of brick can protect us from view but not from bullets.

Figure 7.9: The engine compartment of a car and its wheel hubs offer an effective shelter, while the side panels can be penetrated by bullets.

- A large tree trunk, for example, can be a good shelter. A bush or a hedge, as thick as they may be, offers only cover (*Figure 7.7*).

- A reinforced concrete wall is an excellent shelter. A thin party wall of wallboard or even of brick is a cover that can be pierced by bullets (*Figure 7.8*).

- In the case of a car, it is fundamental to bear in mind that the body, the doors, and the seats generally are not able to stop bullets, whereas the engine and the wheels provide an effective shelter (*Figure 7.9*).

In a civilian defense situation, generally what is needed is a good shelter and almost never only cover; it is very difficult, if not impossible, to be able to lay an ambush against the attackers. Cover might be very useful in getting away from the scene of the encounter while keeping out of sight, but then we are no longer speaking of armed defense; avoiding conflict is obviously the ideal solution when the opportunity presents itself (if we can reach cover and hide from the attackers, it is not advisable, except in cases of absolute necessity, to break from the cover and resume the encounter—naturally in this example we are speaking of civilians, private citizens, and not of professional operators, either public or private). In our technical considerations, we concentrate on the use of shelter properly speaking: buildings, objects, surfaces, elements that are bulletproof, behind which we can take shelter while we return fire. There are three basic types of shelter: high, low, and lateral:

- A high shelter is, as can be easily imagined, any type of shelter that is wide enough to cover our entire body and is high enough to enable us to look and shoot over its top; a small wall of adequate height, a window opening, a heavy, solid piece of furniture, and so on.

- A low shelter does not offer protection to a standing human and forces us to squat down, get on our knees or to lie prone; it could be a low wall less than a yard high, a full barrel, the engine compartment of a car, etc. We have already spoken of the shelter offered by a car as well as the pros and cons of the prone position in the chapter dealing with firing positions. When we take shelter in a kneeling position behind a low shelter, such as the engine compartment of a car, there are those who prefer to stay somewhat away from the compartment to avoid the risk of bullets ricocheting off the shelter's surface itself and then hitting us, or being hit by splinters; nevertheless, as a general rule, uncertainty reigns supreme in a defensive situation, and there may be multiple threats which are not only to our front, and if we have distanced ourselves from the shelter we are more exposed (threats from the sides, from above, etc.), and so we prefer to take maximum advantage of the shelter by staying as close to it as possible.

- A lateral shelter can protect most of our body to a fair degree vertically but forces us to expose ourselves to the side in order to fire; the corner of a building or of a room, a doorway, a tree trunk, etc.

The firing positions (or combat positions) are those that we have already presented and discussed in the preceding chapters; as with any technique, they have to be modified to fit the situation, that is, (in this case) they are tailored to take the best advantage offered by the shelter. When we fire from behind a shelter, it is important to expose as little of our body as possible, to maximize the protection offered and minimize the risk of being hit. For this reason, for example, when firing with a long gun you have to keep your strong arm (the arm whose hand is on the trigger) as close to the body as possible rather than raising your elbow (*Figure 7.10*).

In this book, we concentrate on using the handgun, but the principle is the same: lean out to the minimum extent possible from the shelter (*Figure 7.11*).

Figure 7.10: The proper method of holding a long arm is with the strong arm as close to the body as possible so that the elbow and forearm do not stick out past the shelter.

Figure 7.11a: Use of the side of a shelter.

Figure 7.11b: Use of a low shelter.

Note how, in the Israeli method, the weapon's barrel protrudes only slightly past the shelter. This choice is due to the fact that, if the weapon's muzzle were to remain behind the edge of the shelter, there is a high probability that the muzzle blast would bounce off the surface of the shelter itself and throw powder and fragments into our face, or worse, in the excitement of a real encounter we might make a mistake and fire a shot directly against the surface of the shelter causing an extremely dangerous ricochet that could affect our safety as well as that of anyone else sheltering with us. These are not theoretical examples, as it has happened and continues to happen in reality.

In chapter 10 we will analyze this technical aspect in depth, examining possible objections and their answers. For the time being we will state this concept: the Israeli technique holds that when firing from behind a shelter the barrel of the weapon should project past the shelter, for the reasons we have just explained.

The Israeli school has another peculiarity, speaking of shelters: a shelter is a precious resource, but should not be idolized, and should not be our only and absolute priority, it should not prevent us from taking a correct tactical approach (which implies an effective reaction against the aggressor).

Figure 7.11c: Use of a high shelter, for example an armored car.

In a real-life situation, what happens at the moment we are attacked? Let's imagine an aggressor who starts to shoot at us. If our first reaction were to be to run (let's say to beat a retreat) towards shelter, not only would the attacker's offensive action not be impeded, but it would in fact be made easier. Put yourself in his shoes: would it be easier to concentrate your aim on a fleeing target or one that is shooting back?

That is why the Israeli method always calls for attacking the attacker: even in a military setting, when you are ambushed, the rule is not "everyone take cover" or "every man for himself," but is rather "fire and maneuver" against the attacker. The attacker is put under pressure and is not allowed to carry out his attack freely. This is also a basic thesis that we have already touched upon in the book, and will return to in the last chapter.

Turning again to our "civilian" defensive scenario, in case of an attack, if there is a shelter immediately available, all is well and good, but what we always have to think about is to react against an attacker immediately and put him under pressure, then (in priority order) to take advantage of any shelter that may be available to continue our defense with greater tactical ease. We should not wait to get behind some sort of shelter; we draw our weapon and engage the aggressor with a brief series of shots so as to make him "pull his head in" (and not only metaphorically) after which we can run like lightning to get behind some shelter.

It is important to understand well the sense of these statements and to always be mentally ready and flexible enough to adapt to the situation at hand. If the shelter is immediately accessible (that is, it is only a few yards away, let's say between three to five yards) we can take advantage of it, no question about it, but the availability of shelter should not prejudice (replace) our armed response. If the shelter is very close, we can opt to get behind it while we draw and rack the weapon; rather than just one step to the side, as called for by the basic draw technique, we can take two or three very rapid and aggressive steps in the direction of the shelter so as to be behind it at the moment when we are ready to open fire. But remember: if we don't reply with our own fire, those few yards could be deadly.

It should be obvious, but it is worth noting the following: we prefer (aside from particular instances such as a military combat situation) to avoid shooting wildly while running towards a shelter some distance away. The same applies when we are behind a shelter; never keep your head behind the shelter and expose the weapon and fire without looking. It would be useless, counterproductive, and very dangerous:

- Useless: the probability of hitting an attacker is minimal;

- Counterproductive: we are wasting precious ammunition, we are not hitting the attackers, and then when they close in on us there are only four or five rounds left, so then what do we do?

- Very dangerous: in a real-life situation there are innocent bystanders, neighbors, etc.; how could we even think of firing wildly?

The shelter protects us but is not a cocoon in which we should enclose ourselves. By taking advantage of the protection offered by the shelter we should nevertheless maintain our mobility and our ability to observe the situation and to choose the appropriate actions.

CHAPTER 8

CHANGING MAGAZINES

Statistics are undoubtedly an important frame of reference but, in the context of a subject as complex as the use of a firearm for defensive purposes, the variables can be infinite and difficult to lay out completely. Many of us have probably heard or have read that the average shooting engagement takes place at the distance of a few yards, lasts only a few seconds, and results in only a few shots being fired. It is true that at times a shooting engagement can be over in a very short time and with little ammunition expenditure, but it is not always like that.

A firefight can be a confused, chaotic, prolonged event in which a huge number of rounds may be fired before the situation is resolved in favor of one of the sides involved. In addition, the Israeli school uses methods and principles that stem from the need to defend against the threat of a terrorist attack. The basic tenet of IDC shooting thus calls for carrying several magazines in order to be ready for a long drawn out encounter calling for expenditure of massive amounts of ammunition. A large reserve of ammunition can be precious when facing a threat which from the tactical point of view is very complex (a heavily armed and/or well sheltered attacker, etc.) or having to face more than one threat contemporaneously. It can also happen, especially in the case of a civilian or of an operator who is not psychologically prepared, that the stress and adrenaline of a surprise encounter lead to firing more rounds than necessary.

In summary, under varying circumstances it can happen that during a firefight you can suddenly find yourself with an empty pistol. It is therefore necessary to have spare magazines available and to know how to make a quick, safe, and effective magazine change.

Basic Technique for Changing Magazines (Unloaded Weapon)

During a shooting engagement, as we were saying, it can happen that we expend all of the rounds in our magazine without neutralizing the threat. We then need to change the magazine to replenish the ammunition available to fire.

First of all, how do we become aware that our weapon is out of ammunition? Contrary to what you read or see at times on the screen, in reality during a firefight it is very difficult to keep track of how many rounds we have fired. We become aware, in fact, that the weapon is empty when it no longer fires.

Nevertheless, before taking it for granted that the weapon is in fact empty, we have to check it visually to verify its status (*Figure 8.1*); is it loaded or is it jammed?

Is the slide completely to the rear and the chamber empty? Or have a bullet or a casing jammed somewhere? If we are dealing with a malfunction or a jam of some sort, we have to deal with it (to clear a jam, as we shall see further along in the book,

Figure 8.1: When the weapon fails to fire we have to make a quick visual check (in front of us or to our side) to determine if it is simply empty or if there is some kind of problem (a jam). If it is empty, we immediately change the magazine.

or to change weapon, or to take shelter or run, etc.). If, however, the slide is open and we do not see a jam or other problem, then OK; the weapon is empty and we can immediately change the magazine.

Following is the standard technique for changing a magazine on an empty weapon:

1. The strong hand is raised, bringing the pistol roughly to eye level; it is advisable to raise the weapon rather than to lower your gaze because doing so, while we follow the operation visually, we are able to keep an eye on our surroundings. An unfocused view is always better than no view at all if our gaze is cast downwards (*Figure 8.2*).

2. While the thumb of the strong hand is used to release the magazine catch, the weak hand grasps the bottom of the magazine between thumb and index finger (*Figure 8.3*).

3. With the pistol still raised in front of your face, the weak hand pulls the empty magazine and throws it away and to the rear (*Figure 8.4*); the energy of this action does not depend as much on any practical need (even though it is not a good idea to have an empty magazine underfoot) as it does due to the situation charged with stress and adrenalin. It should be stressed that, in any case, our technique calls for "actively" extracting the empty magazine with the weak hand, rather than letting it fall "passively," even if it is helped with a simple shake of the right hand; in some types of pistols, in fact, the magazine tends to slide out easily once it is released, but according to the Israeli approach it is better to develop the habit of extracting using the other hand. This is because, in the first place, there is no absolute guarantee that the magazine will always slide by itself (it could for example be dirty or defective) and anyway, as we well know, Murphy's Law is lurking, and if the magazine were not to eject on its own, we would find ourselves with a weapon not able to fire and with our weak hand busy with the spare magazine which we have in the meantime pulled out; we would then lose too much time to resolve the situation and to complete loading the weapon. In the second place, we give preference to simple and effective rules which, once assimilated, can work in almost all situations;

Figure 8.2: To change the magazine the weapon is raised to eye level rather than lowering your gaze.

Figure 8.3: The thumb of the strong hand pushes the magazine release while the weak hand grabs the lower part of the magazine.

Figure 8.4: The weak hand extracts the magazine and discards it.

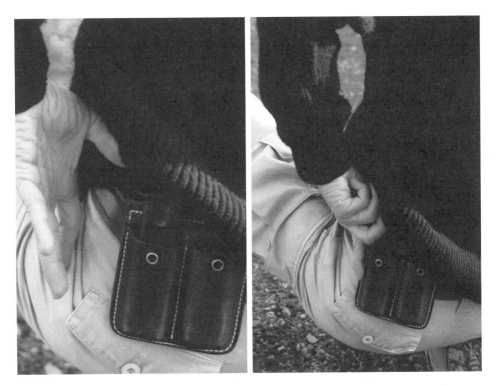

Figure 8.5: The weak hand pulls out a spare magazine (the correct position of the magazine in the magazine pouch allows us to grab it quickly in the most effective manner for the operation).

by making "active" extraction of an empty magazine an automatic response, we are ready and operational with any type of pistol, even if it differs from the type we are accustomed to using.

4. By taking advantage of this same movement, beginning the return move in advance, the weak hand grasps a spare magazine in the magazine pouch, which we have on the same (weak) side. The magazine is grasped between the thumb and middle finger, while the index finger extends along its leading edge (*Figure 8.5*). Naturally, it is important for the magazines always to be inserted properly in the magazine pouch, that is, upside down with the leading edge facing forward; it is a basic rule to ensure a fluid and natural magazine change.

5. The weak hand then brings the magazine towards the pistol. The movement is very simple and instinctive (there is a physiological automatism in which "one hand seeks the other"; our two hands are able to find each other immediately without our having to see them, even in pitch darkness). The index finger extended along the front edge of the magazine increases the ease of insertion into the magazine well; the fingertip allows us to position the magazine more quickly into the well, whereas holding it only by the bottom, without the finger extended, would risk twisting and slowing the insertion (*Figure 8.6*).

6. When inserting the magazine into the opening, the palm of the weak hand pushes it upwards until it is properly seated. The typical "click" of the magazine catch should be heard. Nevertheless, because of stress or because of ambient

Figure 8.6: The index finger of the weak hand, extended along the edge of the magazine, makes insertion easier (if the magazine is held improperly, for example only by the bottom, insertion is much more difficult, especially under stress).

Figure 8.7: During insertion, make sure that the magazine is fully seated (it's a good idea to give the bottom of the magazine a sharp rap).

Figure 8.8: Push the hold-open catch (preferably with the thumb of the weak hand) to close the slide and chamber a round.

noise we might not hear the "click" sound, it is a good idea to give the bottom of the magazine a sharp rap with your palm to ensure that the magazine is firmly seated in the well (*Figure 8.7*).

7. At this point we release the slide, pushing the hold-open catch or pulling it back quickly and decisively, as though partially racking it. Unless we are really expert, both of these actions should be done with the weak hand; the hold-open catch could also be moved with the thumb of the strong hand, but if you are not proficient this could throw off the weapon's alignment and so is not advisable. The thumb of the weak hand should lower the catch while we are reassuming the two-hand grip to be ready to fire (*Figure 8.8*). If however we have some years of experience behind us, releasing the hold open catch with the thumb of the strong (right) hand is so quick and instinctive that it does not compromise operational effectiveness.

8. When the slide closes it chambers a round so that we are ready to fire. (We have to pay attention and not get confused under stress, and rack the weapon as though we were chambering a new round; having closed the slide after inserting the magazine, there is already a round in the chamber, and if we were to rack again, we would eject the round and lose it).

The magazine can be changed while standing, but in order to avoid being static and exposed during a moment of relative vulnerability, it is better to get into the habit of doing it while kneeling. As soon as the weapon ceases to fire, we should always instinctively drop to our knee (it would be even better to be behind a shelter), check the status of the weapon, and if necessary, change the magazine.

It might be advisable or necessary to change magazines under conditions and in positions that are less than "normal"; while moving, lying down, in a vehicle, etc.; we will see how to accomplish this a bit later on, in the next chapter. Let's say that, basically, we can posit five different types of magazine change: while kneeling, while standing still, walking, running, and seated. Naturally there can be many other types and variations in real-life situations based on the circumstances at hand.

Tactical Magazine Change (Loaded Weapon)

In the preceding section we described the so-called "emergency" magazine change, which is considered the standard type of change (let's call it the "default" option, using computer terminology); when we run out of ammunition, we change magazines. Nevertheless, there is another possibility: the so-called "tactical" change, that calls for changing the magazine before it is completely empty.

During a shooting engagement, we might still have several rounds in our weapon, but, finding ourselves in a momentary lull (for example, the initial phase of the encounter is over, we are not facing a direct threat and we are getting ready to face a new scenario such as entering another room or area whose conditions and level of danger are unfamiliar to us), we change magazines, inserting a new one that is completely full so that we can have as many rounds as possible available. We do not discard the magazine which we have extracted, which still has some rounds left, but we place it in our pocket or in the magazine pouch; we might need those few extra rounds, one never knows.

In reality, it is very rare and improbable that a private citizen would have to defend himself, so the situation more typically applies to professional operators engaged in clearing a hostile environment; let's think about terrorist events such as those that happened at the Fiumicino airport in Rome, and at the Vienna airport, the school at Beslan, the hotels in Mumbai, on subways, in public buildings, etc. This type of magazine change could very possibly be appropriate in such situations. But we will not delve deeply into this discussion here because it is outside the scope of this book.

We will limit ourselves to saying that the Israeli school, in general, makes this type of magazine change using the standard technique; extract the partially used magazine (and to quickly stow it in the magazine pouch if there is time, or in your pocket if speed is of the essence) and, then, a spare magazine is inserted into the weapon. This choice is motivated by the fact that, as we have pointed out several times, it is useful to learn and automate a single standardized movement sequence, without too many complications and variations, because it increases the chances of being able to repeat effectively without having to think about it, even under conditions of extreme stress. Other schools call for quickly readying a spare magazine, bringing it close to the weapon and, with an alternate movement, extracting the empty magazine and holding it in the same hand while they insert the new magazine; then they replace the empty magazine into the magazine pouch. We will not take a drastic position saying that one technique is right and the other is wrong; there are many factors in play, which include the specific circumstances as well as the level of training of the shooter. We would advise each reader to try both techniques and choose what is best for him.

Changing Magazines Under Unusual Circumstances

The basic techniques for changing magazines, as described above, are always valid with respect to their fundamental principles (such as use of the weak hand to extract the magazine from the weapon) but are tailored to meet individual circumstances.

If we are walking or running, it is particularly important to keep the weapon raised in front of our eyes in order to maintain a visual check on the magazine change operation without losing sight of the surrounding area so that we can move in relative safety (it would be doubly risky to lower our gaze while moving, first because we would not be aware of the overall surroundings, and second because we would risk stumbling over or running into some kind of obstacle). We again repeat another detail that we have already commented on in the chapter dealing with movements: we can change magazines while we are moving, but if we have to fire shortly after we have changed magazines, we must come to a halt. We always shoot while still, not while moving (unless the situation is exceptional).

If we are lying on the ground, changing magazines is uncomfortable, but we can do it nevertheless. Whether we are lying on our back or on our stomach, the technique for changing a magazine does not differ much from the standard method. Even if we are lying on our strong side (for hypothetical purposes, the right side) the movement is similar to the standard movement; the weak hand extracts the empty magazine from the weapon and discards it, at the same time reaching for the spare magazine which is in the magazine pouch on the opposite side (which is thus exposed and within relatively easy reach). If instead we are lying on our weak (left) side, the operation is not quite as easy; the weak hand extracts the empty magazine from the weapon and discards it, using the elbow of the weak arm we raise ourselves off the ground enough to be able to reach the magazine pouch and push it forward towards our stomach if possible so that it will be accessible in case we have to use a third magazine. At this point we pull out the first spare magazine, insert it in the weapon and continue the engagement.

If we are seated in a chair, in a car, or in another type of vehicle, we have really little space for the movements needed to change magazines, but we can make do. Before we sit down we can move both the magazine pouch (on the weak side) and the holster with the weapon (on the strong side) a bit forward; in practice we make them "converge" towards our stomach. That way, when we assume the seated position, both the magazines and the weapon will be easier to reach, not being pressed between our side and the back of a seat. Naturally our movements will be more difficult and accentuated in order to draw the weapon or get a spare magazine, but it is the best possible compromise between safety and efficiency (for example, we do not keep a weapon drawn and stuck under a leg when we are seated in a car, nor resting somewhere else or stuck on the dashboard, etc.; in case of an accident or something unforeseen, the risk of losing it and not having it close at hand in case of need would be high).

The general principle is always valid: reactivity, mental alertness, and combativeness are more important than abstract techniques. We cannot set down detailed and complete rules for all possible eventualities, and there is no purpose to devising sophisticated techniques which we would not be able to apply under pressure or in an emergency. What we need to do is to adopt some simple and quick expedients and to be always alert and trained to react decisively in all circumstances, even those that are most surprising.

CHAPTER 9

JAMS, FALLS, AND OTHER PROBLEMS

On the battlefield or during any real-life engagement, uncertainty reigns supreme. This is one of the main themes that we have wanted to present throughout this book; we have to develop a combatant's mentality, even before and more than any definitive combat techniques. The brain is the main weapon against the unknown in real-time combat; techniques are only practical aids, as in the ultimate analysis are the weapons themselves.

In addition to the unknowns inherent in an armed confrontation with an aggressor, there are other unknowns of a completely accidental nature; as they say, Murphy's Law is always nearby. In this chapter we will look at some of the accidents that could befall us in less than favorable moments.

Jams

During a shooting engagement, the gun may jam. The cause may be a mechanical malfunction of the weapon itself, or a defective chambered round, or even, in some cases, a less than firm grip on the weapon. It can happen: don't panic, everything (or almost everything) can be put right.

First of all we underscore a recommendation that we have already made in the preceding pages: by and large, if the weapon unexpectedly stops firing, we should immediately assume the kneeling position, moving slightly forward and to the side while lowering ourselves so as to get out of the attacker's line of fire, and check the weapon visually. Why did it stop shooting? Might we have run out of ammunition (and we should then change magazines) or could it be a jam (and if so what type of jam?). Only by looking and making a rapid assessment can we take the appropriate countermeasures. Let's look at the various types of jams and their causes and remedies:

Failure to feed: The cartridge does not chamber. The reason could be that the magazine was not inserted properly and did not travel far enough to engage, or the magazine was initially inserted properly but when putting the weapon in its holster the magazine release was inadvertently pushed, unlocking the magazine, which then moved slightly when the pistol was drawn (just when the weapon was being readied o fire), or during the course of the day our movements somehow caused this partial release, etc. This type of jam can be remedied by a basic move that is useful to prevent various problems. In shooting jargon this move is known as tap-rack-bang (*Figure 9.1*); the bottom of the magazine is slapped with the palm of the weak hand (tap) to push it upwards into the magazine well so that it seats properly, the slide is pulled back smartly (rack) to chamber a round, and we are then ready to fire (bang).

Failure to fire: There is a round in the chamber, we pull the trigger, but the pistol does not fire. The cause might be a defective primer. The problem in this case is also remedied by the tap-rack-bang procedure just described.

Note: Although academically it is appropriate to differentiate between the two previous examples (failure to feed and failure to fire), in operational reality they are very similar. In fact, here is what happens: after having inserted the magazine, the weapon locks but the round does not fire. Under stress, we see that the weapon is locked, but we cannot properly determine whether we are dealing with a failure to feed (no round in the chamber) or a failure to fire (defective round in the chamber). We do not have time to analyze the cause of the problem, nor should we have reason to do so. If the slide is closed and the weapon does not fire, it is a simple matter of applying the same remedy: tap-rack-bang! No doubts, no analysis, no complicated thoughts; under stress we would not be clear-minded enough, and above all, in such a dangerous situation there is no time to lose. One single remedy, to be applied instinctively and instantaneously: that is the most effective method for us.

Figure 9.1: The basic procedure to clear a simple jam: tap (give the magazine bottom a sharp rap with your hand) – rack (pull back on the slide) – bang (fire).

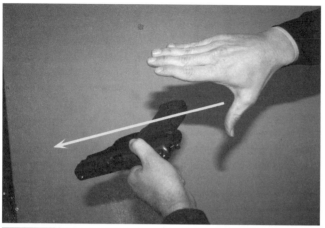

Figure 9.2: To force extraction of a case stuck in the chamber, hold the slide steady with your weak hand and give a strong, sharp push forward with the strong hand on the hilt of the pistol.

We would stress one additional detail: even though our weapon might be a double-action pistol and thus be able to strike an unfired round again, in a real-life scenario it would be useless and counter-productive to try to fire the cartridge by continuing to pull the trigger. If the problem were a slightly defective primer, it is true that on the second or third try the round might fire. But if the cartridge had a serious defect, we would lose time without achieving any result and would expose ourselves to serious risk. It is much better, then, in case of doubt to rack and proceed; we might waste one good round, but we would be ready to fire again much more quickly.

Failure to extract: The round has fired normally but the cartridge case is not ejected (it might be stuck in the chamber because of abnormal case expansion when fired). The slide could remain locked or, more often, partly open, allowing us to see the case still in the chamber. In this case, racking the slide in the usual manner could be ineffective or even impossible; the jammed or stuck casing hinders the movement of the slide and we would not be able to pull it back with the two fingers of our weak hand. We have to take more drastic action; we hold the weapon steady while grasping the top of the slide with our weak hand and then give a sharp push forward on the rear of the pistol grip with our strong hand, as though we were trying to grasp the weapon very tightly (*Figure 9.2*). This enables us to exert much more intense force, allowing us to unlock the slide and expel the cartridge case.

Failure to eject (stovepipe): The round has fired normally, the case has partially extracted but has not completely ejected and is jammed in the ejection port, in a

Figure 9.3: A "stovepipe" jam (failure to eject).

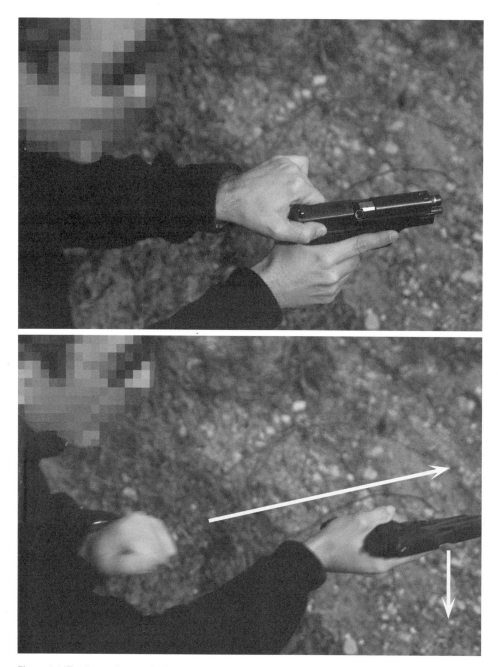

Figure 9.4: To clear a "stovepipe" jam, we rack the weapon while tilting it with the ejection port facing towards the ground.

more or less vertical position. In this position the case looks somewhat like a chimney or a stovepipe (*Figure 9.3*). To clear this type of jam, some schools call for sliding the palm of the weak hand along the top of the slide, starting from the front sight (pay attention not to put your hand in front of the muzzle!) and working backwards; during this movement, the hand hits and frees the jammed cartridge case.

We prefer an alternate remedy: rack the slide, pointing the weapon towards the ground on the side of the ejection port to let the case fall out (*Figure 9.4*). We prefer this method for two reasons: it is an action that in some ways is safer compared to the other (by sliding our hand on top of the slide to free the case we could, under stress, make a mistake—we might not make the move properly enough or we might cut our hand on the edge of the case, and so on); on the other hand, this is always in line with the principle of automating a few essential techniques that are always effective and easy to perform under any circumstances.

Double feed: The case of a fired round remains stuck in the chamber and another cartridge is stripped from the magazine and jams behind the stuck case (*Figure 9.5*). This type of jam is somewhat more complicated than the others. We have

Figure 9.5: A double-feed jam: a case is stuck in the chamber and the fresh cartridge from the magazine is jammed behind it.

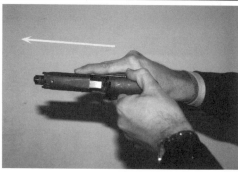

Figure 9.6: To clear a double-feed jam, we have to partially extract the magazine to close the slide, then reseat the magazine, rack to extract and eject the case, and chamber a new round.

to release and partially remove the magazine (that is, let it slide an inch or so without letting it eject completely) so that the slide can close, then re-seat the magazine and rack the slide sharply so as to extract the case from the chamber and chamber a fresh cartridge. At this point we are ready to fire (*Figure 9.6*).

Falls

Even while training at a firing range we might happen to fall; imagine what can happen in the chaotic confusion and stress of a real-life encounter. Blurred vision, tunnel vision focused on the threat, adrenalin exploding, muscles tensed, rough terrain full of obstacles, people running, possibly someone lying on the ground, and so on. It is full of risk of stumbling and falling.

First of all, we will repeat a rule that we mentioned in the previous chapters: always move forward, never backward. To move backward significantly increases the risk of stumbling and falling. Naturally this rule also has its exceptions: high-level training (VIP protection, counter-terrorism tactics, etc.) may include techniques that teach how to back up while engaging the threat.

That said, it can happen that, despite all precautions, you can lose your balance and fall to the ground. In case of a fall, there is only one basic rule to imprint in your memory (including the "muscle memory" that is developed by exercise): while falling, there should be more worry given to keeping the weapon safe than to protecting yourself from the impact of the fall. This means that two essential rules should be followed: keep the weapon pointed towards the target, or at any rate in a safe direction, and keep your finger absolutely outside the trigger guard, away from the trigger. The real danger of an accidental fall is not the impact, but an accidental firing, which could wound us or bystanders. It is better to risk falling badly than letting loose a shot whose consequences cannot be foreseen and which is potentially lethal.

So, if we find ourselves falling, extend the arm that is holding the weapon and keep it taut. Whatever the direction of the fall, orient the weapon in the proper direction (towards the target or towards a safe area) and make every effort to keep it pointed that way; it does not matter much if we are sliding forward or are rolling (*Figure 9.7*). The weapon should never be underneath us (pay attention to not keep your arm bent and pulled in) but neither should it be waved about in all directions. The index finger should be completely outside the trigger guard, resting on the slide. With our other hand and the rest of our body we can try to attenuate the fall, but

Figure 9.7: During a fall it is absolutely necessary to keep the weapon pointed at the target or towards a safe area (and not in contact with our body or waving it here and there) and the index finger must be kept outside the trigger guard, away from the trigger.

our first and only thought should be of our weapon. Only thus can we prevent a problem (the fall) from becoming a tragedy (an accidental shot).

Once the fall has been completed, we quickly assess the situation. Which direction are we facing? Where is the threat? Is the threat still active? Are we in a sheltered position or are we out in the open? Is our weapon ready to fire? Our decision depends on an evaluation of all of these factors: should we continue our defensive action where and how we are (assuming one of the prone firing positions) or should we get up? If the threat is still active but, for example, we are behind some shelter, should we get up to get into a better position? The evaluation is made on a case-by-case basis depending on the circumstances.

The important thing is not to forget to make this assessment instantaneously: thrown off balance by the stress and the fall, if we were to get up quickly without having taken stock of the surroundings we might find ourselves disoriented and helpless in the face of the threat. We cannot know beforehand what the right decision is, because even in the short time it took us to fall we lost control of the situation. While on the ground, then, we spend the first brief moments understanding what the situation is so that we can make the right decision: resume firing while on the ground or getting up on our feet.

A recommendation: even when we get up, we have to be careful to point the weapon in the right direction and keep our finger away from the trigger; be careful, for example, not to rest the hand holding the weapon on the ground using it to push yourself off the ground (contracting the hand could bring the finger into contact with the trigger).

Other Problems

In a real-life combat situation anything can happen: chaos, stress, and the unforeseen reign dominant. Not only are "classic" accidents such as those just described possible, but even the most improbable and unexpected can occur. The answer in all cases is the same: above all, your brain has to work at lightning speed.

An example: we are attacked, and to face the threat we draw our weapon quickly and decisively and… the magazine falls from the well and slides across the ground. It seems like a highly unlikely possibility, but it can still happen: we ourselves have witnessed episodes of this type in a training situation. Perhaps the magazine was not fully inserted and did not seat properly, or maybe the weapon was in its holster and the magazine catch was inadvertently pressed (because of a slight pressure, a bump on the side, etc.). But we don't have time to stop and think about the causes and fret over our bad luck; we are faced with the danger of a real and immediate threat and have to react immediately. What should we do? Bend down to pick up the magazine that has fallen, or ignore it and grab a spare magazine from the pouch? Usually, as a general rule, it is best to choose the second option: grabbing and inserting a spare magazine is usually a much quicker, immediate, and automatic action (if we have trained ourselves well) rather than searching around for the original magazine, which has ended up who knows where. After having fired with the new magazine, if the threat is neutralized or temporarily inactive, we can worry about retrieving the original magazine so that it does not get lost and wasted. Naturally, during all of these goings-on the priority is to never lose sight of the threat and of the overall situation (for that reason you should not lower your gaze to look for the magazine that fell), and deciding just what to do next.

This is only one example, but there could be endless others, because the variables are infinite: "what if...? what if...? what if...?." It is impossible to foresee and categorize every possible surprise that we may run up against, and it is therefore impossible to develop a set of fixed rules to deal with them. If we were to try to develop such a set of rules, the result would be nothing more than an illusory list that would be falsely reassuring. Our answer is always and only this: train the brain to be able to choose, in the moment, on a case-by-case basis, the best solution (knowing however that there is never an absolute guarantee of success). It is not techniques that enable us to face the unexpected, but rather it is only our brain, if we keep it well trained, combative, and alert.

CHAPTER 10

"WHYS" OF THE ISRAELI SHOOTING METHOD

In this final chapter we want to address some of the more frequently asked questions that are posed by those who are exposed for the first time to the Israeli method of shooting (which will also allow us to summarize and condense in a few pages the salient points of the philosophy and techniques described in the book; clearly this involves repeating some of the points we have already made, but this helps us to assimilate them in greater depth and in a more critical sense).

These questions address curiosity or legitimate doubt, in large measure understandable and dictated by good sense, and whose answers are to be found in the strictly operational nature of the methods and techniques to which this book refers (as in general is all of the experience and formative approach of the Israeli school when it comes to security matters); as we have stressed from the outset, these are techniques that have been developed and refined over decades, filtering the data and experience of thousands of real operators and cases, in the name of an approach that is aimed exclusively at defense and combat, at survival in critical and chaotic situations.

We believe that it is interesting to take an analytical look at the ten most frequently asked or representative questions: we have collected them over the years through direct contact, during courses and in various work and other venues.

Each question is discussed at length, seeking to present it in the most detailed and accurate manner possible, without forcing or trivializing any subject (which, we repeat, always deserves to be treated with respect) and is followed by the appropriate answer, which we hope we have also provided objectively and with sufficient clarity.

In short, this final chapter follows the typical FAQ (Frequently Asked Questions) outline. Here, then, are the ten "Whys," or the ten Israeli shooting FAQs.

(*Note*: For anyone who is interested in more detail, any other question not included in this list will be welcomed and we will try to provide an answer through the web site indicated in the book).

1. Working With an Empty Chamber

QUESTION: "Isn't carrying a weapon with an empty chamber a limiting factor? In case of unexpected need, isn't too much time lost racking the slide and chambering a round? And what happens if the hand that is not grasping the weapon is not free (because it is holding a briefcase, a railing, a person that is being protected or held, etc.)? Isn't there a real risk of being slowed down or even being unable to react with the necessary quickness?

ANSWER: Based on the Israeli experience, to adequately answer this question it is indispensable to examine it from many aspects. We have spoken of it in various parts of the book, but it is appropriate to summarize here an answer that touches upon various aspects of the question.

The choice of working with an empty chamber is not an abstract and absolute choice, but is tied to very real considerations concerning the context in which it is posed. The choice derives from a careful balance of risks and advantages, or in other words, costs and benefits.

If the context is that of a private citizen (who owns a weapon for sporting or home defense reasons) or that of an institutional operator who carries the weapon on a daily basis for service reasons (military, police), in our "normal" civilian context, the probability of an encounter involving shooting is enormously lower than the probability of mistakes or accidents while managing and storing the weapon, as statistics and media reports unfortunately remind us of with tragic frequency. Let's think of an ordinary citizen or even of a policeman or military member; how many armed encounters does he have to deal with on average every day? The question itself is absurd; fortunately, even the probability that he would have to face one in his entire life is remote (and hopefully that will always be the case). But this same citizen, police officer, or soldier leaves his house or barracks every morning and returns in the evening, and each time he has to pick up and return his weapon and handle it in the presence of family members or colleagues; how many accidents could happen if he always had a round in the chamber? The answer is, unfortunately, superfluous.

In this daily context it is much better to put safety concerns (as we have amply discussed in the appropriate chapter) above the concern for immediate use. Let us remember, however, that in terms of reaction speed, the act of racking the slide and chambering a round while drawing the pistol slows down engagement of the threat by only a fraction of a second. This can be shown by data and objective measurements, and requires only the proper training of the operator. There are also particular techniques to rack the slide with only one hand in an emergency situation.

Not only that: there is an ample case history of shooting encounters during the commission of terrorist acts (in airports, hotels, crowded places) during which the reaction of Israeli security agents who work with an empty chamber was immediate, effective, and resolute, and instances where other operators (who worked with chambered rounds and the safety on) have not achieved results that were as effective or, even worse, ran into problems and wounded innocent people because of the difficulty in handling weapons under conditions of extreme confusion and stress.

If, however, the context is special and particularly "critical," with a high risk of a firefight and/or with a high probability of encountering problems while drawing the weapon (such as during a VIP protection detail) and/or with an offensive rather than a defensive approach (for example, while raiding a hostile location, etc.), then the Israeli school calls for working with a round in the chamber. Obviously, we are dealing with radically different conditions compared to the everyday conditions that this book refers to, and these would have to be dealt with in a separate venue.

2. Grasping the Weapon

Q: "I have noticed that according to the Israeli style of shooting the pistol is held particularly tightly by the hands and with the thumbs bent, tensed, and overlapping each other; isn't the grasp taught by other schools that call for grasping the weapon with the thumbs extended and pointing towards the target (almost as if you were aiming a rifle) more ergonomic and effective? Doesn't that position allow better control of the weapon and a more accurate aim?"

A: Based on Israeli experience, grasping the weapon with the thumbs closed and overlapping allows the greatest degree of control, keeping it tight as if in a vise, both while firing as well as in any close-range encounters in which there is also a second attacker involved (who may try to disarm us), in a crowd that is confused or has panicked (people who might bump against us or grab hold of us), while firing with one hand, etc.; these latter are circumstances in which it is easy to lose your hold of the weapon if you do not have an extremely tight grasp of the weapon (*Figure 10.1*).

In addition, under stress it is natural that the muscles tend to tighten, and therefore this method of grasping the pistol is fully consistent with the human body's instinctive reactions.

In the third place, we should not forget that the Israeli defense method is based on the concept of combat and not of shooting; we have established that this method of grasping the weapon is the most effective way to transition seamlessly from a shooting encounter to hand-to-hand combat, using the weapon (in case of need) as a bludgeon.

In summary, grasping the weapon with tightly closed thumbs has no disadvantages, even though (in the worst of cases) it might be superfluous or (in most cases) be only advantageous.

Figure 10.1: Grasping the pistol with the thumbs closed. The two upper images are taken from film clips of actual police actions (the officers were wearing body cameras) and you can see how, under stress, it is natural to keep the thumbs tightly closed over the weapon so as to wrap around it and hold it tightly as if in a vise. The two lower images are taken from a film that shows a technique used to disarm someone; if the weapon is held with the thumbs extended alongside the frame, it is very easy to pull it from the hands of the operator without him being able to offer any strong resistance.

3. Standing Firing Position (A): Unnatural?

Q: "Isn't the typical standing firing position, facing full front and with the legs spread, which is taught by the Israeli school, too tense and rigid? Isn't it tiresome to assume, has little flexibility, and is overly forced, almost as though it were a martial arts pose?"

A: Based on the Israeli experience, the point is that it is not a shooting position but rather a combat position. There is no rigid, abstract, impermeable barrier that separates combat with a firearm from hand-to-hand combat. Combat is combat (and self-defense is only one aspect of it). The position adopted in the Israeli school is a combat position because it puts us in a condition to be able to react in a 360-degree arc under all possible circumstances and modes. It allows us to quickly open fire against threats at a distance, to pass quickly to a physical encounter against any close-in aggressors, to run to a shelter or towards an escape route, and so on. We could say that it is a "general purpose" combat position, valid for a wide range of situations and circumstances, and adaptable to almost any unexpected needs.

In addition, the experience gained from actual combat teaches us that, far from being a "forced" and "artificial" position, it is a position that is extremely consistent with the human body's instinctive reactions when faced with a serious and unexpected danger. As we have already explained in the book, when passing from a state of quiet to a state of alarm and defense, the human body tends to tense, pull in on itself, widen its stance to be able to deal with the attack or to run (in the technical sense, of the so-called fight-or-flight phenomenon, a typical automatic response by the nervous system under extreme stress), to pull the head down into the shoulders, remaining facing forward in order to keep both eyes focused on the threat and ready to take in anything that is happening within the widest possible field of vision. The Israeli combat position is a logical derivation and optimization of this instinct.

Do we need further proof? Many other shooting schools teach a much more erect position, with the legs almost extended, not to mention non-frontal positions such as the Weaver position and its derivatives. But let's try to take a careful look at a few film clips of situations of actual danger, in which a police officer finds himself suddenly having to defend himself against unexpected fire from a suspect (and not a situation in which a police officer is engaged in an offensive action, actively chasing an armed suspect, which psychologically and tactically is a much different scenario). There are many such film clips on the Web. Studying them carefully we can see that when faced with such a predicament, the policeman's instinctive reaction is to assume a position very similar to the one we are speaking of, and very different from the standing shooting position (upright and relaxed) that he was taught while training at a firing range. It is the power of instinct, which when exposed to conditions of danger and extreme stress tends inevitably to bypass certain techniques that are not instinctive. Scientific research cited in books by Siddle and Grossman show that, under combat stress, agents trained to shoot in assymetrical positions spontaneously assume a roughly symmetrical and frontal position in more than ninety percent of cases (*Figure 10.2*).

Figure 10.2: Under conditions of extreme stress due to an unexpected deadly danger, the human body tends to instinctively assume a position similar to that which is optimized and taught in the Israeli combat school. The images show police officers who, under the stress of defending themselves, assume an analogous position (quite different from that which they are normally taught).

4. Standing Firing Position (B): Dangerous?

Q: "Isn't the typical standing firing position, facing forward and with legs spread, which is taught by the Israeli school, actually too forward-facing? Isn't it dangerous to expose all of the front of your body to your enemy?"

A: Based on Israeli experience this worry is, on the one hand, irrelevant, and on the other, misleading. It is irrelevant because under actual combat conditions, to expose your flank to the source of hostile fire does not represent much of a significant problem for the attacker. It is misleading because, while it does not offer a significant advantage, assuming a side-facing position against an attacker has several serious disadvantages. It is not an instinctive position and thus runs counter to the human body's automatic defense reactions (see above). It makes you lose time, sacrificing precious movements and moments to respond to fire quickly. It cuts our field of view in half. In addition, in some cases it can increase rather than decrease risk; if we are wearing ballistic protection (a bulletproof vest), our flanks are our most vulnerable spots.

5. Standing Firing Positon (C): Static?

Q: "Isn't the typical standing firing position, facing forward and with legs spread, which is taught by the Israeli school, too static? Isn't it a somewhat impractical position if you have to make quick displacement moves?"

A: Based on Israeli experience and on the physiology of the human body, exactly the opposite is true. It is easy to find very enlightening comparisons and examples. Let's think about some particularly dynamic sport, such as tennis or volleyball. Let's imagine (or better yet, watch a film clip) of an athlete who gets ready to counter a quick and powerful hit, like a serve or a spike: what position does the athlete assume to be able to react with a lightning move? A fully erect position with his legs upright? Absolutely not.

When preparing to deal with the incoming ball and to respond with the maximum force and speed, the athlete spreads his legs as though he were rooting himself to the ground so that his feet are planted as firmly as possible; he bends by flexing his knees to charge himself like a spring; he orients himself to face the source of the incoming ball head-on, pointing both eyes in that direction. A similar position is

Figure 10.3: A position like the Israeli combat position (left), knees bent and legs spread, corresponds to the maximum readiness position that in many sports is assumed by a player who is getting ready to counter a powerful stroke (such as a serve or a spike in tennis or volleyball) and/or who has to spring forward very quickly. In contrast, a standing position, with legs upright and relaxed (on the right) is typical of a resting position or of concentration required for target shooting (not for combat shooting).

also seen in athletes who are getting ready for a speed event, such as speed skating or sprinting (in that case the introduction of starting blocks has led to a "specialist" position, with the athletes leaning so far forward that they have their hands on the ground, but originally the position was analogous to that which is still in use for skating). You can see some examples in *Figures 10.3* and *10.4*.

Still further: let's think in particular of a combat sport, like fencing or boxing. Typical of these sports is an alternating rhythm: there are static phases of closing in on or taking stock of the adversary, and dynamic or explosive phases of attack or defense. If we carefully observe films of these sports, especially if they are of high-level competition, what do we notice of the athletes' positions? What we see is a factual norm: in the static phases the body is erect, with the legs upright, and taking relatively slow and careful small steps; however, in the dynamic phases of attack and defense the body tenses and the center of gravity becomes lower, with the legs flexed, spread, full of tension, ready for lightning-quick action.

Figure 10.4: Several examples of athletes "ready to jump" in different sports. The common denominator is the positon of individuals ready to react with explosive energy (someone ready to deal with the incoming stroke): legs spread and tensed, lowered center of gravity, facing the direction of the incoming stroke. Just the same as the Israeli combat position.

In summary, a position with our legs spread and "spring-loaded" is highly reactive, while (to the contrary) a position that is too upright and relaxed is not at all in keeping with the needs and explosive reactivity typical of self-defense and of combat. It is not by chance that under critical stress combat conditions even someone who has been taught to use the upright position tends to assume an "Israeli-style" instinctive position (see question 3 above).

6. Kneeling Position

Q: "It seems to me that the Israeli school teaches only one kneeling position (gluteus resting on the rearmost foot, chest erect, arms extended towards the target); isn't it too far back, static, and "hybrid" compared to two different kneeling positions taught by other schools? These other schools have a "dynamic" position leaning forward towards the target (without resting on the rearmost foot) as well as a position seated on the rearmost foot with the elbow of the supporting arm resting on the forward knee (to make aiming easier); aren't two positions preferable, each tailored to a certain target or a certain situation?"

A: Based on Israeli experience, the kneeling position they have opted for is preferable because it embodies the best possible combination of stability, comfort, and effectiveness. As we have described in the book's technical chapters, this position enables us to best maintain our balance and control of our firing even if we are bumped or pushed, and at the same time allows us to point (or if necessary, aim) as accurately as possible. In this case, and let us not forget it, we are also dealing with a combat position, not just a shooting position (*Figure 10.5*).

While not questioning their motives, the kneeling positions taught by other schools, based on our experience do not guarantee such a degree of balance: for example, in the forward-leaning position, if the operator is bumped or pushed he immediately loses his balance and has to take precious seconds to regain it; in the more compact seated position the shooter's body is under tension that cannot be maintained for very long (also, depending on their body structure, many people would not be able to assume the position properly in the first place). In both cases, however, these are firing positions rather than combat positions, because they are mainly geared towards accomplishing aimed fire and not towards being able to react to a 360-degree threat under all circumstances.

In addition, considering the importance of capitalizing upon and maximizing the human body's instinctive reaction to a threat, the Israeli school holds that it is highly advisable to learn one kneeling position well, so that in any situation the operator is ready to assume it immediately without having to stop to think about choosing from a number of alternatives. Finally, it is obvious that depending on specific circumstances, even the Israeli kneeling position should be adapted to the situation at hand; if for example you are shooting from behind a low barrier, such as a car's engine compartment,

Figure 10.5: Top photo: The kneeling firing (or more precisely, combat) position typical of the Israeli school. The lower photos show two different kneeling positions taught by other schools.

naturally it will be impossible to have your buttock resting on the heel of your trailing foot, so you will modify the position. As we continue to repeat, these are not hard and fast techniques, but pragmatic solutions that always have to be guided by the needs of the moment and the operator's intelligence.

7. One-Handed Firing Position

Q: "I don't understand what sense there is to the typical Israeli one-handed firing position, with the other arm extended up and to the side. I have heard many different explanations but none of them convince me… In any case, isn't it a uselessly showy position?"

A: Based on Israeli experience, this is not a "choreography" for its own sake, because the Israeli way does not accept anything that is superfluous; everything that is done is based on very precise technical reasons and on careful study of a great number of real cases. No movements are allowed in pursuit of aesthetics, but only of practicality. As we have explained in this book, the reasons for this position are substantially as follows: balance and stability; protection (from or of other people); ability to quickly rejoin both hands to continue the shooting engagement.

Sometimes it can happen that the target is so close and/or at such an angle that you cannot grasp your weapon with both hands after having racked the slide; the threat came as too much of a surprise, or was too far to the side of our position, and so forth, so that we reply to the fire as quickly as possible as soon as our own weapon is pointed in the right direction, without waiting those fractions of seconds required to join the weak hand to the strong hand. It is normal that the weak hand rests slightly away from the body.

In other cases, it might be advisable to keep other people who are in the area at a distance (a person we are protecting, passersby who have panicked or who are confused, or even a second attacker who should be kept at bay for a moment before we "busy ourselves" with him); there are other valid reasons why the weak arm should be extended off to the side.

The Israeli experience has shown that other ways of positioning the weak arm during one-handed shooting, for example with the weak hand held against the chest, or downwards, or holding your belt, etc., offered no special advantage, and in fact could turn out to be useless or even counterproductive (for example, when it is needed to maintain balance and a safe distance in the midst of a crowd). To the contrary, the position we have described here has proven to be particularly effective in operational situations.

Once again we repeat this principle: the technical choices assimilated in the Israeli school are the fruit of a large practical case history, and not of theories dictated by aesthetic tastes or by abstract criteria.

Figure 10.6: The one-handed shooting position according to the Israeli school; the speed of the encounter or the position of the body do not allow firing with two hands, so the weak arm assumes a "support" position, ready to deal with people nearby (be they friendly, neutral, or even hostile).

8. Firing from Behind Shelter

Q: "I have seen that according to the Israeli school, when firing from behind shelter, generally the weapon is exposed outside of the shelter itself; isn't that dangerous? Doesn't it force you to expose yourself excessively, and above all doesn't it run the risk that a second attacker, hidden on the other side of the shelter, might be able to wrest the weapon from me or hit my hand with a club, and so forth? Wouldn't it be better to stay completely behind the shelter?"

A: Based on Israeli experience, in a real combat situation the risk is very high that, due to stress, whoever is firing from behind a shelter, close to the shelter wall itself, might hit the wall by mistake or might fire so close to the wall that it could cause a ricochet, with serious consequences (wounds to the face or eyes, panic, etc.).

In simulations at the range, if you fire close to the walls used as baffles, you may see that often they vibrate noticeably because of the gases from the muzzle blast; if instead of wood or plastic barriers these were masonry walls, the shooter would be hit by a significant amount of particles and debris. Even worse, during the excitement of a real encounter, a major error in pointing the weapon (because of instinctive fear of exposing oneself too much or because of the movement of the weapon while firing) could lead involuntarily to firing a shot at the wall itself, causing a very dangerous ricochet of the bullet.

To fire from behind but close to a wall thus exposes us to risk even during training, even before any actual shooting situation, and brings to the fore the question of shooter safety. As a consequence, the Israeli school has chosen to fire by extending the muzzle of the weapon past the wall in order to avoid such a risk (*Figure 10.7*).

With respect to exposure, in the technical chapters of the book we have explained the Israeli approach, which we can summarize in the following terms. First: in case of attack, our priority is to react to the threat and to put pressure on it; if there is shelter available, very well, we should certainly take advantage of it, but the priority should not be to fall back and think only of taking shelter, the priority is to fight. Second: when we take advantage of shelter, our rule is "expose yourself as little as possible, protect yourself to the maximum," whatever is necessary to avoid being hit and to continue to fight, but in a real operational situation, in a real firefight, it is not possible to take the time to measure inches or fractions of inches. Therefore our approach is: fight and take shelter, depending on the situation at hand. We fight with

Figure 10.7: In the photo on the left, the position of firing from behind a shelter used in the Israeli method: the weapon sticks out past the edge of the shelter. In the photo on the right, the shooter is backed away from the shelter. In this case the obvious smoke from firing should be noted within the walled area (observing the actual firing sequence one would even be able to see the obvious shaking of the partition due to the muzzle blast); if this were a masonry wall, there would be an extremely high probability that chips and powder would fly in the shooter's face, not to mention that under stress a mistake in aim could result in a ricochet.

our brain and our pistol, not with a yardstick or a protractor.

The other objection, concerning the possible presence of a second attacker on the other side of the wall who is ready to attack us or take our weapon from us, in our opinion is not logical from the tactical point of view. We are speaking, in fact, of a scenario in which we are sheltering behind a wall because on the other side there is an armed attacker (let's call him attacker "A") who is either shooting at us or is capable of doing so. In such a case, how could an accomplice (who we will call attacker "B") be close to the wall precisely in the area towards which "A" is shooting or aiming? And, even worse, how could "B" reach for our weapon to wrest it from us, placing himself precisely in the line of fire between us and "A"? We are not aware of any attackers with those kinds of masochistic tendencies.

It is obvious that, if there is no attacker "A" on the other side of the wall, but we are only checking out a room in which we do not know if there is a threat, we would adopt a different tactic, ready to poke the weapon inside the instant it was necessary to shoot.

9. Quick Changes of Position

Q: "I have noticed that in rapid displacements according to the Israeli style they are almost always carried out in a manner characterized by quick rushes alternating with strange almost "jumping" halts; isn't that type of halt a waste of energy and time compared to more "normal" and spontaneous movements?"

A: Not according to the Israeli experience. In fact, it is the most appropriate technique for stopping quickly and in tight spaces while maintaining equilibrium or being able to reestablish it very rapidly. On the other hand, to stop "while sliding" or in one pronounced lurch itself exposes us to a high risk of sliding and falling, especially on unstable ground (that might be covered with water, ice, gravel, oil, etc.).

If we think about it, the principle, as well as the subjective sensation we feel, is similar to an automobile's ABS brake system. When we brake with a car equipped with the ABS option, our foot instinctively tends to "lock down." If we were to lock down on the brake pedal of an older generation car the wheels would lock instantaneously and the vehicle would slide forward. With ABS, however, even if you were to push on the brake pedal to the limit, the wheels do not lock but instead make a series of controlled rotations which become progressively shorter, thus avoiding sliding. The sensation experienced by the driver, who keeps his foot pressed to the pedal, is of a controlled and "jerky" braking sequence. This system results in safer braking in a shorter space.

Figure 10.8: The typical "Israeli-style" full stop consists of stomping your feet on the ground like pistons so as to slow down and stop in the shortest distance possible without losing your balance, even on wet, icy, or otherwise slippery ground.

10. Moving Towards the Threat

Q: "I have seen in many videos (both of exercises and of operational actions) that the Israelis undertake a shooting engagement in reaction to a threat, rather than to pull back to remove themselves from the threat or to quickly find shelter, and they tend instead to move towards the threat or even to rush as quickly as possible towards the attacker or attackers; isn't this a simply foolish and dangerous act?"

A: In line with the experience and spirit of the Israeli combatant, which always seeks to apply (even under stress) the proper tactical assessments, the key to dealing with an armed threat is to react with the utmost aggressiveness, without going on the defensive (which in general leads to suffering the consequences of the attack and making the attacker's task easier). We have to transform ourselves immediately into the predator. Attacking the attacker means that we put the psychological and physical pressure on him (or them). Let's try to imagine the following situation. A hunter is on safari. He finally spots his prey, a lion, lying in the vegetation. We will now look at three different ways in which the event could unfold.

First variant: The lion is not aware of the hunter's presence. The hunter aims his rifle, controls his breathing, takes aim, and fires. The lion falls dead.

Second variant: The lion becomes aware of the hunter and changes position, moving to the side through the bushes. The hunter has little time to fire, and in addition has to evaluate the lion's movements. It is more difficult to take aim calmly, but the only variable that puts the hunter under pressure is the relatively greater difficulty in aiming and firing.

Third variant: As soon as the lion sees the hunter, it charges towards him with powerful, quick bounds, covering yard after yard in a few fractions of a second. You can be certain that even the most experienced hunter will probably feel an adrenalin rush in his veins, have his heartbeat go wild, become short of breath, and have his hands shake. Under these conditions it will be very difficult for him to shoot calmly and accurately, and he runs a serious risk of turning from the role of predator to that of prey.

Do you think that this is a theoretical and fanciful example? Try searching the Web (for example, YouTube) for actual film clips using keywords such as "lion charging hunter" or "lion attacking men" or something similar; you will find truly impressive video documentation. A few frames are provided in *Figure 10.9*.

Figure 10.9: Let's put ourselves in the hunter's shoes: we are the aggressor, the animal is the prey. Here we see some frames from actual film clips taken from the Web (unfortunately the image resolution is typical for such cases).

In the first sequence (the upper sequence) we first see the lion in a position of wariness, behind the bushes, and then when he is charging at a full run; in which of these two conditions would we feel calmer and more focused on a shot?

In the second sequence (the middle grouping) we see how a large group of hunters is surprised and frightened by the lion's charge, to the point that they are not able to stop the lion before it jumps on one of them.

In the third sequence (on the bottom) a tiger charges out of nowhere and attacks a party hunting for an elephant without anyone being able to stop him.

These are three concrete examples of the psychological effects of pressure put on an aggressor (the hunter) whose prey has become the predator; and to say that in these cases the "prey" is not even capable of responding to the fire....

Figure 10.10: Predators can be put to flight by a combative prey who, although theoretically inferior physically and/or numerically, takes them by surprise and overturns their psychological and tactical advantage. This is true not only in nature, and not only in military situations, but also in daily life.

It is not by chance that we see this approach in Israeli military tactics. A patrol or a convoy moving along a road in an open area, or possibly between hills or buildings, falls into an ambush; armed attackers fire from the sides of the road, from the tops of the hills, or from inside the buildings. How should the soldiers react? Should they try to distance themselves from the hostile fire, should they try to seek shelter by bunching up behind or under their vehicles? That would be the best way to fall victim to the attack, taking substantial losses. According to Israeli doctrine, the most effective tactical reaction is this: reply to the fire and advance towards the attackers, reducing the distance, putting them under pressure and driving them off. Fire and maneuver, fire and maneuver, covering each other while everyone moves towards the threat. Never the prey, always the predator.

As even further proof, we would like to cite a final episode, which is truly curious but also very noteworthy. It is a case which happened just as this book was ready to go to press and was reported to some extent by the mass media, given its uniqueness. It might seem to be almost a joke, but instead is absolutely real. The protagonist this time is not a lion or a soldier, but a little old lady. The headline: In England an old lady chases off a gang of thieves by hitting them with her purse (*Figure 10.10*).

It might make us laugh, but it is an authentic episode and is very appropriate to our discussion. A gang of young thieves is attacking a store; the owner and sales staff have barricaded themselves inside and the thieves are smashing the windows to grab what they can. Bystanders are watching from a distance, intimidated and passive. Suddenly an old woman comes upon the scene and, with unrestrained fury, begins to hit the thieves. The surprise is complete, and the psychological situation has been reversed so that the thieves (who suddenly switch from the role of unchallenged aggressors to victims) are not able to coordinate any kind of reaction and flee. They run off in such a chaotic and hasty manner that two of them fall with their scooter and at that point are overcome and held by the crowd (which takes action, having gained some courage following the attack by the old lady). Few other episodes could better typify or demonstrate this principle that we have repeated and discussed many times. Never remain as the prey, always attack the predators. It works.

In conclusion, here is an eleventh answer, to a question that is rarely asked and is always implicit and hidden in the background:

Q: "But why, given so many alternatives, should we follow the Israeli way?"

A: Our objective as we have made clear at the beginning of the book, is not to set forth a thesis such as "Follow the Israeli way because it is the absolute best way," but instead is to invite the reader to discover its merits. Each reader is able to explore and understand a series of principles, both philosophical and methodological, as well as technical, that he can, if he wishes, integrate into his own knowledge base and his "menu options." Our hope is that all of this might be useful in the unfortunate event that we are forced to face such a situation. We have no commercial purpose in this, or of competition or rivalry. As the saying goes, we are all on the same side of the fence, along with anyone else who works either professionally or personally in the field of security and defense. We all must contribute to safeguarding that fundamental value that unites us: protection of human life against threats that, unfortunately, are present and numerous nowadays. We hope that we have succeeded in furthering that intent with this book.

We do not wish to claim, therefore, that the Israeli way is necessarily better than or superior to any other. But at the same time we feel that it is important and useful to be aware of it for at least two reasons.

First reason: This is a method and a combat school that can claim a long and deep experience, in the contemporary era, given the problems and often tragic turn of events regarding the security situation in Israel and the Middle East (both in the military and law enforcement fields). It is an experience, moreover, that is marked by its high success rate in all situations and scenarios. Few other combat schools, probably, would be able to claim a comparable degree of proven effectiveness in the field on an almost daily basis. For this reason military and civilian operators who work in high-risk areas often attend specialized courses in Israel or courses taught by Israeli instructors. And it is also for this reason that Israeli operators in the private security field, especially in "hot" areas, are the most expensive, normally at the top end of the cost scale.

Second reason: The social, political, legal, and civil situation in Israel is much more similar to that in Europe and some other countries than it is in the USA. Aside from extreme "border" situations, the lifestyle, relationship with weapons and their use, the pertinent laws, the type of urban and living environments, and many other aspects of daily life in Israel are very similar to those in European and extra-European countries where ownership and use of firearms are far more regulated than they are in the USA. As a consequence the Israeli approach to defense shooting is naturally more consistent with its requirements and scenarios. But even in the USA, naturally, the Israeli techniques can be usefully studied and integrated because of their effectiveness.

CONCLUSIONS

Everything we have spoken about in this book is a wealth of knowledge and techniques that is constantly evolving, and is open to future developments.

As we have said, the Israeli method is born of an operational experience that has matured in the field, in a long historical journey, and from scientific studies that constantly support it and refine it. This procedure is, by definition, unending; as it has happened in the past, and as it is happening today, it will also continue to happen in the future.

New scenarios, new cultures, new operational requirements can determine modifications and updates to everything that we have described in the preceding pages. All of that, however, should not be considered as a fixed, frozen, and crystallized subject, but rather, should be viewed as flexible, malleable, to mold as necessary, as long as there continues to be a need for security and defense of human life against violent attacks.

Shalom!

Fabrizio Comolli

Fabrizio Comolli has for years been involved in armed and unarmed defense training courses with SDU and collaborates with the team on many projects. He has a background in humanities (with degrees in philosophy and psychology), and an in-depth professional experience in the editorial and communications fields, but he also nurtures a parallel interest in the fields of security and defense (having practiced combat disciplines for twenty-five years, in particular Muay Thai, street fighting, and Krav Maga, and is a personal defense instructor). He manages the Combat series for Edizioni Libreria Militare.

SDU (Security and Defense Unit)

SDU (Security and Defense Unit) is a specialized, high-end instructional team in the field of strategic and tactical security, of defense and of combat (the Israeli School). The members of the SDU team have over twenty-five years of experience in operational activity in security services in Israel and Italy. They also have a specific curriculum as instructors, having completed a rigorous training program called for by the Israeli school.